PHILIPPIANS

Triumph in Christ

PHILIPPIANS

Triumph in Christ

by

JOHN F. WALVOORD

MOODY PRESS · CHICAGO

© 1971 by
THE MOODY BIBLE INSTITUTE
OF CHICAGO

Library of Congress Catalog Card Number: 78-143473

ISBN: 0-8024-2050-8

Fifth Printing, 1974

CONTENTS

5

INTRODUCTION

ALTHOUGH NOT THE LONGEST or the most important of the Pauline epistles, the letter to the Philippians has its own peculiar charm and important place among the epistles of Paul. Written with Ephesians, Colossians, and Philemon as one of the prison epistles, it breathes the rare perfume of Christian joy and peace in a context of suffering. Combining the practical with the theological, the triumph of the life in Christ—even for one who is in great suffering—is offered for those who have the life of Christ.

In writing this present commentary on the epistle to the Philippians, the author, who previously published an exposition of the epistle under the title *To Live Is Christ,* has attempted here a completely new work based on the exegesis of the Greek text, but designed for general reading and study. Like all other commentators on the epistle to the Philippians, the author is indebted to the great works of the past, especially to the incomparable exposition by J. B. Lightfoot, whose eloquent English, thorough scholarship, and devotional spirit delight every reader. Yet, a fresh study written in the context of a modern world in the light of contemporary, practical, and theological problems offers a challenge to any expositor. If this writing exalts the Lord Jesus and makes the Word of God more precious, the author's goals will have been realized.

In a modern world overrun by secularism, unbelief and materialism, and too often satiated with the unparalleled luxuries of modern life, a letter written by a prisoner in chains may seem at first glance to be irrelevant to our contemporary scene. A careful study of this epistle, however, revealing the amazing triumph of the apostle even though in great suffering, soon removes the veneer of modern superficiality from our present world, and brings the reader face to face with ultimate spiritual values, which satisfy the heart and bring joy and peace in a way that no modern convenience or pleasure could duplicate. [For those seeking depth in spiritual things, a real intimacy with Jesus Christ, and a life that counts for eternity, this epistle offers infinite treasures]

OCCASION

About ten years before the writing of the epistle to the Philippians, the apostle Paul had visited Philippi, as recorded in Acts 16:12-40. Prior to coming to Philippi, Paul had had the unusual experience of being forbidden by the Holy Spirit to preach the gospel in Asia, and was told not to go into Bithynia (Ac 16:6-7). After proceeding to Troas, seeking the guidance of the Lord, the apostle saw in vision a man of Macedonia beseeching him, "Come over into Macedonia, and help us" (Ac 16:9). He concluded from this "that the Lord had called us for to preach the gospel unto them" (Ac 16:10). Sailing from Troas, they had come to Philippi via Samothracia and Neapolis, the seaport of Philippi. In light of the fact that Europe was later to become the cradle of Christianity and the fountainhead of missionary effort throughout the world, the strategic character of this penetration of the gospel into Europe was as important as his later visit to Rome.

The unusual success of the apostle in winning early con-

verts in Philippi, his experience of being beaten and imprisoned, and his miraculous deliverance all served to etch
deeply on the memory of the apostle this strategic advance in
the preaching of the gospel in the first century. The apostle
was later to visit the church twice in A.D. 57, about five years
after his first visit. And now, after another five years, during
which there had been apparently frequent contact with the
church by means of letters or messengers, this important
epistle is addressed to the church, already somewhat mature
in the faith after ten years of growth.

The immediate occasion of the epistle was a gift which
had come from the church at Philippi, brought by Epaphroditus (Phil 2:25; 4:14-18). Epaphroditus, after reaching
Paul, had suffered a serious illness which almost caused him
to lose his life. Now recovered (Phil 2:26-28), he was about
to return to the Philippian church. With him Paul intended
to send this letter. It was far more than a mere word of
thanks for their thoughtfulness and love. From the deep
wells of apostolic affection, the apostle draws this rare revelation of his own heart for the Philippians and his exhortations
for their spiritual progress.

AUTHORITY AND DATE

Conservative scholarship has been almost unanimous in
asserting the authorship of the apostle Paul as stated in 1:1,
and supported by much early evidence attesting the genuineness and integrity of the epistle, as well as the authorship of
Paul. Among early extrabiblical supporters of Pauline authorship is Clement of Rome in his *Letter to Corinth,* Igna-
tius in his *Letter to Smyrna,* Polycarp in his *Letter to Philippi,*
Irenaeus, Clement of Alexandria, and Tertullian.[1]

Generally speaking, those who have challenged the genuineness of the epistle have been radicals such as Baur, Volk-

mar, Holsten, and the Tübingen School. As H. C. Thiessen
and many others have pointed out, the arguments against
the authenticity of this epistle quickly pale into insignificance
before the genuineness and warmth of its Pauline revelation.[2]
Those who have accepted the genuineness of the other
Pauline letters have little problem with Philippians, either
in its content or its structure.

The date of the letter has been variously argued and depends upon the order of the prison epistles and the place of
writing. If the imprisonment of Paul began about A.D. 58-
60, and was terminated before the burning of Rome in A.D.
64, the epistle must logically have been written sometime in
this period. Some have considered the other epistles written
from prison (Ephesians, Colossians, and Philemon) as occurring first. However, if Lightfoot is correct, and his arguments are forceful, the epistle to the Philippians was
probably written first, about a year after his arrival at Rome,
and therefore approximately A.D. 62 or 63.[3]

The date of the epistle is, of course, linked to the question as to whether Paul had two imprisonments. The commonly accepted conservative position that there were two
imprisonments with a brief period of ministry between has
been debated at length; but, in any case, the probability is
that the epistle to the Philippians was written before Paul's
case was tried and at the close of the two years referred to
in Acts 28:30.

The book of Acts records a number of imprisonments of
Paul, such as that in Philippi (Ac 16:23-39), Jerusalem
(Ac 21:33—22:30), Caesarea (Ac 23:23-35), and the
imprisonment in Rome from which the epistle to the Philippians was written (Ac 28:16-31). F. C. Synge supports an
imprisonment in Ephesus based upon the reference in 1
Corinthians 15:32, "If after the manner of men I have

fought with beasts at Ephesus," and other references such as 2 Corinthians 1:8-11; 6:5; 11:23. It is also claimed that Paul avoided Ephesus on his last journey to Jerusalem (Ac 20:16-17).[4]

Of the four possible imprisonments in addition to Rome, those at Philippi and Jerusalem did not offer circumstances in which a letter could be written, and it is also unlikely that this would take place in Caesarea. Why is Ephesus taken seriously inasmuch as there is no specific imprisonment mentioned there?

The crux of the argument in favor of Ephesus hangs on the interpretation of the word "praetorium" in Philippians 1:13, translated in the Authorized Version "the palace," and in most revisions "the praetorian guard." It is argued that the word "praetorium" really refers to a building, that is, the government house such as would be the residence for the governor of a province. Hence, Pilate's residence in Jerusalem was the praetorium (Mt 27:27; Mk 15:16; Jn 18:28, 33; 19:9), and there is reference also to the praetorium in Caesarea where Paul was kept (Ac 23:35). This is the argument advanced by Synge.[5]

Further, it is pointed out that there is no government house in Rome because it is actually the capital, and therefore does not need a provincial government house.

Donald Guthrie offers the best statement of the argument in favor of Ephesus, although he himself finally concludes that the Roman theory has the most supporting evidence. Among the problems of a Roman origin of the letter and in favor of Ephesus, he cites the problem of receipt of gifts for the Philippians which would have been very easy at Ephesus, near Philippi, but difficult for faraway Rome. The proposal of visiting Philippi also seems more plausible if coming from Ephesus. The argument that there was frequent com-

munication between Paul and Philippi also would favor a
location nearer Philippi itself instead of Rome, which is
about eight hundred miles away.

It is also argued, as Guthrie points out, that difference in
literary style and language of Philippians as compared to
the other early epistles might indicate that it was from a
different period. Some also feel that Paul's controversy with
the Jews would fit better at Ephesus than at Rome, and that
finally there seems to be some disparity between the circumstances of Paul's imprisonment in Rome and what one would
expect from the epistle itself. As Guthrie points out, however, "the cumulative effect of this evidence is undoubtedly
strong, but it falls short of truth . . . it seems better to give
the preference to Rome as the place of dispatch."[6]

However, strong evidence exists against considering this
a reference to either the government house or the barracks
where the guards stayed, another possible meaning. As
J. B. Lightfoot points out in an extended debate, the word
"praetorium" properly means the praetorian guard as translated in many revisions. To contend as Synge does that
there is "no evidence that the word was used in Rome in this
sense" is arguing from silence.[7] The fact is that the phrase
"and in all other places" (better translated "and to all
others") seems to refer to people rather than places and
would tend to confirm that the praetorium referred to the
praetorian guard rather to a palace or government house.

The total context of the Philippian epistle suits Rome
much better than it does Ephesus, and coincides with a specific reference in Acts 28:16, where it indicates that Paul
actually came to Rome, and in Acts 28:30 that he lived in
his own hired house even though under guard. There is no
question about the Roman imprisonment, whereas there are
serious questions concerning the Ephesian imprisonment in-

asmuch as the entire argument is based on inferences rather than expressed statements of the Scripture. It is for these reasons and many collateral arguments brought out by Lightfoot, Hendriksen, and others that the majority of conservative scholars consider Rome the most probable place.[8] Although Hendriksen places Philippians as the last of the prison epistles rather than the first as Lightfoot does, he cites a dozen arguments in favor of the Roman origin of the epistle.

Accordingly, in this exposition it is assumed that the letter came from Rome and the chronology which this supports will be assumed as correct. Suggestions that the epistle to the Philippians may have come from Caesarea or Ephesus lack sufficient evidence to be taken seriously. The context of this epistle seems clearly to be Rome with its reference to Caesar's household (4:22).

Lightfoot also gives an extended treatment of the meaning of Caesar's household, refuting several false conclusions drawn from this, and finding it another genuine reference to Paul's residence in Rome.[9]

PLACE OF COMPOSITION

The importance of the context of this epistle as written from Rome, the capital of the Roman Empire, has been expressed forcibly by Lightfoot in his long chapter on St. Paul in Rome.[10] Although arriving in Rome as a prisoner, his presence there, like his first visit to Philippi, was most important for the extension of the gospel. As the central city of the entire Roman Empire, no more strategic place for a faithful gospel witness could be imagined. Years before his arrival a large colony of several thousand Jews had been taken from their native land to Rome by Pompeius. As Lightfoot points out, they soon established themselves in a quarter of their own, were given friendly treatment by the earlier Caesars, and rapidly grew in number and influence to the point that Seneca complained about their political influence.[11] According to Acts 18:2, Claudius is said to have expelled the Jews from Rome, but this was either temporary or not fully executed, as their stay in Rome seems not to be seriously affected.

It was to this colony of Jews that Paul had earlier sent his epistle to the Romans, the most comprehensive theological statement of any of his epistles. This letter had been sent about A.D. 56, and had been written at Corinth during the three-month stay of Paul there (Ac 20:2-3).[12] Paul did not arrive in Rome until some four years later; and although most of the Jewish colony were cool to him, he found some friendly Christians awaiting his arrival (Ac 28:15).

Once Paul was firmly established in Rome, according to Acts 28:17, he lost no time in calling together the leaders of the Jewish community to whom he pleaded his case and asserted his innocence (Ac 28:17-20). Their noncommittal reply, asserting that they had received no letters about him from Judea, paved the way for a later appointment at which Paul expounded his point of view. As in other Jewish communities, however, there was a divided response to his teaching. Although there had been many rumors of false Christs which had preceded Paul's announcement, and though undoubtedly there was an attitude of expectancy on the part of the Jews, they were not prepared for Paul's gospel. As Lightfoot expresses it, "But the Christ of their anticipations was not the Christ of St. Paul's preaching. Grace, liberty, the abrogation of the law, the supremacy of faith, the levelling of all religious and social castes—these were conditions which they might not and would not accept."[13]

There soon developed among them some strong antagonists to Paul, some of them non-Christians, and others professing Christianity but not agreeing with Paul's doctrine of grace. These opponents, as Paul testifies in Philippians, made his lot harder (1:15-16) but this only encouraged him in his faithful witness to the Gentiles (Ac 28:25-28), and served also to strengthen his friends who were encouraged by Paul's resolute stand for the gospel (Phil 1:14).

Paul's circumstances in Rome formed an unusual context for his ministry there. Although allowed some freedom to preach (Ac 28:30-31), he probably was chained by the wrist to a guard twenty-four hours a day (Ac 28:20; Eph 6:20; Phil 1:7, 14, 16; Col 4:18; Phile 1, 10, 13). No doubt some of the guards, who were regularly changed every six hours, were friendly and tolerant, while others could be most abusive and foul in their language and attitude. To a person as sensitive as Paul, to whom being alone with God would have been the highest privilege, such constant association with men so calloused to human feelings and so indifferent to his welfare must have been a real trial. Yet this very occasion permitted Paul to have an audience which could not escape, which saw in his life the transforming grace of God, and heard from his lips the amazing testimony of how he had come to know Christ. The constant daily association of guard and prisoner soon wore through the veneer of sin and cruelty, and softened their hearts; and one by one the guards seemed to have come to know Christ. Through them the gospel soon was preached to others and, as these Christian guards were sent to the ends of the empire on various missions, the gospel went with them.

Paul's circumstances in Rome could have been worse. Apparently, as a Roman citizen, he was granted some unusual privileges such as living in his own rented house (Ac 28:30), and his friends seemed to have had free access to

him. Little mention is made of these friends in the epistle
to the Philippians, but that there were many Christians
known to him in the area is clear from his earlier epistle to
the Romans with its many greetings in chapter 16. Close to
him were Luke and Epaphroditus; another close friend,
Aristarchus, is mentioned in Colossians 4:10. Others who
shared fellowship with him in his captivity were Tychicus
(Eph 6:21; Col 4:7); Epaphras (Col 1:7; 4:12); John
Mark, who was now restored to fellowship with Paul (Col
4:10; Phile 24; cf. 2 Ti 4:11); and Demas, later to desert
him but at this time still faithful (Col 4:14; Phile 24; cf.
2 Ti 4:10).

Another person known to us only through Colossians
4:11 by name of Jesus (also called Justus) apparently was
one of the faithful Jews who stood by Paul when other Jews
forsook him. The book of Philemon adds Onesimus, a slave
who had run away from home, as another in Paul's circle of
friends. It seems quite clear that the life of Paul, although
confined, was not a lonely one without Christian fellowship.
As trying as his confinement must have been to his restless
and ambitious soul desiring to preach the gospel, his pulpit
could not have been more effective or more far-reaching.
As a prisoner he was penetrating into a community and
preaching to individuals who otherwise might have been
untouched by the gospel of Jesus Christ. Paul's circumstances provide another illustration of God's providence
turning tragedy into triumph and a prison into a pulpit. The
far-reaching effect of his ministry is alluded to in subsequent
Roman history, as here and there prominent individuals are
found who seem to have given their heart and life to Christ.

ADDRESSES

If the epistle to the Philippians was written from the most

important city in the Roman Empire, it was also written to a church located in a strategic area of Christian testimony. Lightfoot in his extended treatment of "the church of Philippi" points out the unusual importance of this city, made a Roman colony a century before Paul.[14] Located on the important trade route between Europe and Asia, it was the gateway to both continents, situated in a depression of the mountain barrier which elsewhere separated Europe and Asia. When Paul arrived with Silas and Timothy in A.D. 52, the city already had a great history, dating from its founding about 357 B.C. by Philip II, father of Alexander the Great. Although its rich gold and silver mines had already been thoroughly exploited, the soil was still rich and its commerce extensive. It was a strategic place for a Christian church as travelers passing back and forth would come in contact with the gospel and, if converted, would carry the news to their ultimate destinations.

The unusual experience of Paul in meeting with the comparatively few Jews in this town who, according to Acts 16:12-13, were accustomed to gather at the riverside for prayer, forms a background of the epistle. It was there that the first convert in Europe, a woman named Lydia from Thyatira, was won to Christ. This early triumph was followed by the casting out of a demon from a damsel and the resultant riot and imprisonment of Paul and Silas (Ac 16:16-24). The painful circumstance of the apostle in prison in Philippi became a platform from which the gospel could be preached. Loosed from his bonds by the earthquake, and keeping the jailor from killing himself, Paul witnessed the birth of the Philippian church with the conversion of the Philippian jailor and his household and their immediate baptism.

These never-to-be-forgotten experiences in Philippi were

the beginning of a warm friendship between Paul and the Philippian church which apparently was cultivated by repeated contacts prior to Paul's imprisonment in Rome. Lightfoot cites the many evidences of these contacts in the period from A.D. 52 to 57.[15] In that year Paul seems to have paid two visits to Philippi (2 Co 1:16; Ac 19:21; 20:1-3, 6). Lightfoot feels that the epistle to the Galatians was written from Macedonia at this time.[16]

No further mention of the Philippian church was made until Paul arrived as a captive in Rome. Their love gift at the hands of Epaphroditus, who had been sent by them to Paul, aroused great joy in his heart and was the immediate occasion of the epistle. After the incident of Paul's writing this letter to Philippi, little is found in the Bible or elsewhere concerning the Philippian church. The few scant mentions give little insight into the state of the church. Although in Paul's day it was an outstanding testimony to Christian love and fidelity to the gospel, Lightfoot sadly comments, "Of the church which stood foremost among all the apostolic communities in faith and love, it may literally be said that not one stone stands upon another. Its whole career is a signal monument of the unscrutable counsels of God. Born into the world with the brightest promise, the church of Philippi has lived without a history and perished without a memorial."[17] Lightfoot, however, is speaking with more eloquence than facts, as there are still impressive ruins of the church at Philippi today. The whole area actually became uninhabited in the course of time. Although the church did not long survive, the letter addressed by Paul to it has accomplished what no temple on earth could memorialize. The truth of God stands when stones decay and human hearts defect.

INSPIRATION AND CANONICITY

The place of the epistle to the Philippians in the inspired Word of God and its recognition as canonical by the church have both been well attested. As previously pointed out, except for radical critics, few have dared to attack the epistle's authenticity; and if genuinely from the pen of Paul, as even some liberals concede, its divine inspiration becomes apparent.

The contents of the epistle with its high degree of evidence for divine inspiration is to all sensitive souls the supreme evidence for the genuineness and inspiration of this letter of Paul. The church, in recognition of this, has uniformly included the epistle to the Philippians in all of the early lists of canonical books. There does not seem to have been any challenge to its place in the Scriptures in the early church. As Lightfoot states, "The Epistle to the Philippians appears in all the CANONS OF SCRIPTURE during the second century: in the lists of the heretic Marcion and of the Muratorian fragment, as well as the Old Latin and Peshito Syriac versions."[18] There is less reason to challenge Philippians than probably any other book in the New Testament. Guthrie declares its genuineness is so commonly recognized as to render discussion unnecessary.[19]

CHARACTER, CONTENTS, AND THEOLOGY

As the context of the epistle indicates, the letter to the Philippians did not originate in the desire to correct any doctrinal variance or any serious moral problem in the church. The letter predominately was designed to express the joy and love of the apostle Paul and his heartfelt appreciation of the love of the Philippian church which was manifested in their gift to him. Although containing many exhortations to deeper Christian experience and warning against possible dangers, including exhortation to a closer love within the Philippian church itself, on the whole the epistle is a letter of experience rather than doctrine. Yet it also contains some of the most important theological utterances to be found anywhere in Paul's writings, such as the *kenosis* passage in Philippians 2. The letter is a direct outgrowth of the manifested love of the Philippian church rather than a polemic such as the epistle to the Galatians, which was addressed to a serious error.

Because it is directed to those already achieving a high level of Christian experience, it is all the more intimate and relevant to Christians seeking a deeper life. The constant exhortations to rejoice, to increase in love toward the brethren, to avoid any shadow of schism or lack of unity, and to achieve the ultimate in peace and joy and fellowship in Christ are important themes of the epistle.

As the epistle develops, the triumph of the apostle's own sufferings is introduced in chapter 1 as a portrait of one who is truly magnifying Christ. Collateral illustrations are given in chapter 2, including the important reference to Christ as an example of triumph in Christian experience and dedication reproduced in the lives of Paul, Timothy, and Epaphroditus, who are used as illustrations. The triumph of the believer in Christ walking in fellowship with God is outlined in chapter 3; and the present possibility of peace—peace in the heart, in the church, and in respect to circumstances—as the believer is strengthened by Christ—forms the concluding chapter.

The epistle is related more emotionally than theologically to its human author and, although rich in revelation of God and His ways, provides an intimate window into Paul's own heart and experience. Even the sharp break in Philippians 3:1, when Paul seemingly was about to conclude his epistle, obviously was prompted by love rather than theology, and motivated by the desire to make Christ supremely the object of their faith and devotion. To attack the epistle as if this break indicates a combination of two previous manuscripts is unjustified, and most conservative scholars have agreed that the epistle as it is has a literary unity even if its logical progression is not as methodical as the epistle to the Romans. It is a love letter of a fond parent for his spiritual child, coming from the heart more than the mind of Paul. Yet it contains the loftiest revelation, the most intimate insight into deep spiritual truth, and supremely exalting Jesus Christ as the object of the believer's faith and devotion. Few literary efforts, whether Scripture or otherwise, are more richly rewarding to the careful reader.

The epistle's theological importance is apparent in its constant repetition of major doctrines of the faith: the remainder of salvation by grace, the emphasis upon present spiritual experience of victory in Christ with joy and peace, and the ultimate eschatological hope of standing perfect in Christ in resurrection or translation; all important truths in their theological implications. The great statement of the *kenosis* of Christ found in Philippians 2:5-11 is probably the supreme theological utterance of the book, stating profoundly and yet simply the fact that God became man, the nature of His condescension in emptying Himself, taking the form of a servant, and assuming the likeness of a man, ending in the supreme humiliation of dying on the cross. Coupled with this historic record of how God became man and died is the equally remarkable exaltation found in resurrection, an exaltation of Jesus Christ as Lord to which every tongue must some day give recognition. These central facts of theology are the heart of all the experience and hope which is expressed so beautifully in this epistle. If one had no other book but Philippians in the New Testament, and all else had been lost, most of the essentials of true faith in Christ, true Christian experience, and abundant hope would still be documented.

RELEVANCE TO MODERN CHRISTIANITY

The modern world, and with it the modern church, has been afflicted by unbelief, secularism, and materialism which have deteriorated its faith, clouded its vision, and cluttered its life with the temporal. The timeless relevance of the Word of God as a whole is illustrated effectively in this epistle to the Philippians written so long ago. Today as never before a believer in Christ needs to have a clear vision of his Saviour, an intimate walk of fellowship, the inner peace and power that come from such association, and the unclouded hope of the life to come with its resurrection from the dead, its glorious body, and its fulfillment in the presence of the Lord. Coming from the context of the triumph of its human author suffering in prison for Christ's sake, limited in earthly things, and yet overflowing in spiritual power and joy, the epistle is well adapted to speaking to human hearts tender toward Christ and willing to listen to His revealed truth. It is an epistle to be read often, worthy of long meditation, and one which provides spiritual healing for those wounded by the present world. It is the triumphant Word of God for those who would triumph in Christ today as it was for those who triumphed yesterday.

1

TRIUMPH IN SUFFERING

THE WARM, INTIMATE RELATIONSHIP of Paul and Timothy
to the church at Philippi is indicated in the absence of apostolic titles, also omitted in the two letters to the Thessalonians and Philemon. As Marvin R. Vincent expresses it,
"The character of the whole epistle is reflected in this introduction. It is unofficial, affectionate, familiar, unlike the
opening of the Galatian Epistle, and more nearly resembling
the introductions to the two Thessalonian letters."[1]

Since Paul's first memorable visit to Philippi about A.D.
52, there had been many friendly contacts as both Paul and
Timothy had visited the church frequently. Paul had been
there twice in A.D. 57.[2] Timothy also had been at Philippi
several times (Ac 16:1-3; 17:14-15; 19:22; 20:3-4; Phil
2:19-23). The church had ministered to Paul's physical
wants (2 Co 11:8-9; Phil 4:15-16), and just prior to the
writing of this epistle had sent another love gift to Paul
through Epaphroditus (Phil 4:15-18). Probably no other
church provided the loving fellowship and thoughtfulness so
encouraging to Paul in his prison experience.

Instead of claiming apostolic office and title, Paul and
Timothy are described simply as "the servants of Jesus
Christ," literally slaves of Jesus Christ. Although in Phile-
mon Paul calls himself "a prisoner of Jesus Christ" (Phile

1:1), and in Romans and Titus he refers to himself as a slave in addition to the mention of his apostolic office (Ro 1:1; Titus 1:1), only here is the expression used alone in the salutation of Paul's epistles. Significantly, he takes the same place as Timothy who had had such an effective ministry in Philippi. Timothy is mentioned with Paul in seven epistles: 1 and 2 Corinthians, 1 and 2 Thessalonians, Philippians, Colossians, and Philemon. Timothy, who was with Paul in Rome during most of his imprisonment, is omitted only in Ephesians in the prison epistles.

The letter is addressed "to all the saints in Christ Jesus which are at Philippi." The expression "saints" is a general designation of those dedicated to God, and therefore holy or sacred; hence, reserved for God and His service. It is used both for angels and men.[3]

The mention of bishops and deacons indicates the advanced state of organization of the church at Philippi now composed of mature and gifted believers from whom recognized leaders had come. As A. R. Fausset notes, "This is the earliest epistle where bishops and deacons are mentioned, and the only one where they are separately addressed."[4] Of course, as early as Acts 6, men were appointed in the church to serve in a way similar to deacons. Although not called deacons, the prominence of this appointment of men to special service in Acts seems to recognize its significance. Elders were appointed in every church as early as Acts 14:23, and are mentioned in Acts 11:30; 20:27-28; 1 Thessalonians 5:12-13.

As Calvin and most commentators since have understood it, the address to bishops and deacons is evidence that a bishop is equivalent to a pastor or teacher, and that a deacon usually is the one in charge of charity and temporal things in the church. As Calvin states.

The titles, therefore, of *bishop* and *pastor,* are synonymous. And this is one of the passages which Jerome quotes for proving this in his epistle to Evagrius, and in his exposition of the Epistle to Titus. Afterwards there crept in the custom of applying the name of *bishop* exclusively to the person whom the presbyters in each church appointed over their company. It originated, however, in the human custom, and rests on no Scripture authority.[5]

The custom of appointing bishops and deacons was characteristic of the early Christian communities.[6] While not mentioning his own apostolic office, Paul extends the courtesy of recognition to these church leaders, and with it a subtle suggestion that the unity of the church (which seems to have been threatened) could be maintained by proper recognition of leadership.

After the epistle is introduced with the usual salutation found in all of Paul's epistles, the apostolic greeting is extended, "Grace be unto you, and peace, from God our Father, and from the Lord Jesus Christ." The words "grace" and "peace," wonderfully significant of the Christian's relationship to God, beautifully express the content of Christian salvation and the triumph of Paul in suffering, which is the theme of chapter 1. In grace, the unmerited favor of God toward those who have trusted in Christ is revealed, and with it the whole sustaining power of God for the Christian is embraced. The result is "peace," peace with God through Jesus Christ, and the peace of God, the inner, supernatural tranquility which is produced as the fruit of the Spirit (Ro 5:1; Phil 4:7; Gal 5:22). Although a customary form of greeting, it expressed the longing of Paul's heart that the Philippians would realize to the full the wonderful provision of God for both grace and peace.

The general form of verses 1 and 2 follows the custom

of the first century in writing letters. Such correspondence usually begins with the name of the writer, and Paul follows this custom in all of his letters. After the name of the writer there is usually an expressed prayer or wish for the well-being of the person receiving the letter. This is often followed by a brief statement of what is being communicated. While the body of the letter often differed, it usually closed with a prayer or benediction. The form of Paul's letter, therefore, is not unusual; its content and inspiration set it apart. Archeological discoveries confirm that Paul's letters were similar to the letters of others. As J. H. Harrop points out, letters were used not only for ordinary social purposes, but to express philosophic, scientific, and other literary productions, some having more rhetorical character and more definite plan than others, as illustrated in the epistle to the Romans.[7]

THANKSGIVING FOR THEIR FELLOWSHIP IN THE GOSPEL, 1:3-8

Philippians, like 1 Thessalonians, which is a letter of appreciation for the faithfulness of Christians in Thessalonica, is essentially a thanksgiving for the work of grace in Philippi, and for their thoughtfulness in sending Epaphroditus with a gift to Paul in prison in Rome. With a full heart he writes, "I thank my God upon every remembrance of you." Paul's heart was filled to overflowing as he reviewed in his mind how God had worked in Philippi in leading them to salvation, in forming the church, his own sensational deliverance from jail at Philippi, the subsequent development of the church, and their kindness to him on many occasions. The Philippians were constantly in his prayers, and an unfailing source of joy and satisfaction (v. 4).

The apostle's prayer life is a remarkable aspect of his total testimony and is frequently mentioned in his epistles (Ro 1:9; Eph 1:16; Col 1:3, 9; 1 Th 1:2; 2 Th 1:11; Phile 4). In his busy life on his missionary journeys as well as now in his imprisonment, Paul dedicated many hours to prayer. In our modern day when program and publicity and promotion characterize the Lord's work, it is sometimes overlooked that without prayer no eternal work can be accomplished for God. Paul's prayer life is a noble example to all who would be effective in Christian work and testimony. No doubt the Philippian church had also prayed for him, and this forms part of their fellowship with him. He mentions, "your fellowship in the gospel from the first day until now" (v. 5). Their fellowship was not only social and spiritual, but they were fellow laborers through their prayers and gifts in all that Paul had wrought, as he states in Philippians 4:15-16.

Significant in the early verses of this epistle is the reference "to all the saints in Christ Jesus" (v. 1), and "you all" (v. 4). One of the problems with which the apostle deals in chapter 4 is a minor rift in the church; it was of a social rather than a theological nature, and Paul was seeking to heal it on the basis of their common love for him and for the Lord. The word "all" is repeated twice in 1:7 and again in 1:8. The fact that he can thank God for each one of them sets a high standard for relationship between a pastor and his people, whether in the first or the twentieth century. Many pastors would have difficulty thanking God for everyone in their flock.

His joy in their present fellowship is matched by his confidence in the certainty of their future perfection at "the day of Jesus Christ." This expression, which occurs three times in Philippians (1:6, 10; 2:16) and three times in Paul's other epistles (1 Co 1:8; 5:5; 2 Co 1:14), is probably a

reference to the day when Christ will come for His church
(1 Th 4:13-18). If so, it is used in contrast to "the day of
the Lord," which contextually refers to the time of judgment
and the millennial kingdom of Christ on earth. The day of
the believer's perfection will be the day of his translation
or resurrection. Meanwhile, Paul is confident of God's continual working in them. Having saved them, God would
complete His work of grace in their future deliverance and
glorification.

Paul's confidence in God and in the Philippians has sound
basis in the past evidences of their faith mentioned in verse
7. He declares his confidence is fitting "because I have you
in my heart," and "in the defence and confirmation of the
gospel, ye all are partakers of my grace." An alternate translation, "because you have me in your heart," as Lightfoot
points out, is not supported by the order of words in the
original.[8] His reference to "in my bonds, and in the defence
and confirmation of the gospel," is not evidence that his trial
had already begun. It is rather that the Philippians had
shared his suffering, as well as his labors, and had been partakers of the same triumph over suffering made possible by
the grace of God.

In these seven verses of introduction, an amazing expanse
of theological truth had already been introduced. The words
"servants," "saints," "grace," "peace," "prayer," "joy," and
his expression of confidence, thanksgiving, and hope constitute an impressive background for the rest of the epistle.

The apostle's thankfulness for them, his joy in their fellowship, his confidence in their ultimate spiritual triumph, and
his assurance that they are partakers of the grace of God
only serve to increase his love for them. Paul calls upon God
to record how greatly he longs after them in the compassions
of Christ. He yearns for them as a mother for a child. He

mentions that Epaphroditus had the same feeling toward them (Phil 2:26). His longing for them was born of the Spirit who had produced the fruit of love in Paul's heart. As F. B. Meyer expresses it, "The Apostle had got so near the very heart of his Lord that he could hear its throb, detect its beat; nay, it seemed as though the tender mercies of Jesus to these Philippians were throbbing in his own heart."[9] Having the heart of Christ and His compassion transforms all human relationships; places love on a supernatural plane; enables us to love the unlovely, the unthankful, and the indifferent; and impels us to prayer. This is the heart and compassion of God supernaturally implanted in the human breast. This compassion is further expressed in the following passage which reveals Paul's deep concern for them.

Prayer That They Might Be Filled With the Fruits of Righteousness, 1:9-11

The fruit of the love and compassion of Christ finds its highest expression in prayer. Having mentioned his thankfulness and joy as he prays for them in verses 3-5, Paul declares that the content of his petition is fourfold. In his first petition he prays that their love "may abound yet more and more." How often the Scriptures remind us that love is the primary quality of Christlikeness. It was this quality which should distinguish disciples of Christ from all others (Jn 13:35). Love is the first of the fruit of the Spirit, without which all the other fruit loses its luster (Gal 5:22-23). It is the greatest of the three great virtues—faith, hope, and love (1 Co 13:13), and the indispensable quality to every spiritual gift, whether it be tongues, prophecy, faith, sacrifice, or martyrdom (1 Co 13:1-3). Too often in listing theological fundamentals of the faith, love as a fruit of the Spirit is omitted. It is actually the sine qua non of Christianity today,

as well as in the Philippian church. Particularly because
there had been a rift in the spiritual fellowship of the Philippian church, alluded to in 4:2, the great need of the Philippians, like the church of Ephesus in Revelation 2, was to
return to their first love (Rev 2:4).

In this, the only possible standard is love which continues
to abound increasingly. Such love, however, is more than
just emotion. It is love rooted "in knowledge and in all
judgment." The word for love is *agape,* the deepest word
for love in the Scriptures. The knowledge to which love is to
lead is, as Lightfoot expresses it, *"advanced, perfect knowledge."*[10] Here it means spiritual knowledge, theological
knowledge, the comprehension of the total revelation of
God concerning Himself, man and salvation. It is only as
we comprehend the love of God toward us, unworthy as we
are, that we can in turn love those who are imperfect. Then
he adds, "in all judgment" (the word occurring only here in
the New Testament), referring to *"feeling," "perception,"
"insight,"* and *"experience."*[11]

As Lightfoot expresses it, "Love imparts a sensitiveness
of touch, gives a keen edge to the discriminating faculty in
things moral and spiritual."[12] As knowledge deals with general principles, so perception and insight deal with its application.

The love for which he is praying is that which comes from
the heart of God who is omniscient, infinitely discerning, and
fully aware of all the deficiencies of His creatures, and yet
is impelled to love because He is a God of love. Such love
cannot be static, but must abound.

In his second petition in verse 10, Paul logically proceeds
from his prayer for love abounding in knowledge and in
judgment to the corresponding quality of a discriminating
sense of values expressed in the clause, "that ye may approve

things that are excellent." The idea of approval comes from a word meaning "to examine carefully" or "to test." The conclusion "that are excellent" more literally means "to discriminate between things that are good and bad," or things that are opposed to each other. Spiritual discernment sorts all things out as good or bad in the sight of God determined by divine rather than human criteria. An accurate translation would be, "that ye may discriminate between things that differ." The same expression occurs in Romans 2:18 where it speaks of knowing God's will and of being instructed out of the law. In a world which has lost its sense of value, a Christian must have unusual sensitivity to what really counts.

Such discernment leads to the third petition of Paul, "that ye may be sincere and without offence till the day of Christ." By "sincere" is meant they would have purity of motive, a purpose in life obviously pure and unsullied by selfishness, sin, or worldly standards. The Greek word translated "sincere" is usually considered to be an interesting combination of two words referring to sunlight and judgment, indicating the genuineness of anything examined in the full light of day. Such sincerity in motive leads to a life that is without offense to God or man when judged by God's standards. The desire of the apostle is that the motivation of the Philippians in their service for God would stand the searching test of judgment at the climax, the day of Christ, the day of their resurrection or translation.

The fourth petition of the apostle is that the Philippians would be "filled with the fruits of righteousness which are by Jesus Christ." This is a summary statement gathering in all that has preceded—their love, their discernment, and their being without offense. To these spiritual qualities must be added all the other "fruits of righteousness," an Old Testament expression (Pr 11:30; Amos 6:12) also used by

James (3:18). The fruits of righteousness which are mentioned are those which come from their relationship to Jesus Christ rather than to the law (Phil 3:9).

The fruits of righteousness comprise evidences of transformed character by the power of the Holy Spirit, and the resulting works of righteousness which fulfill the will of God in the individual life. So, it is a holy life and a holy character manifesting the fruit of the Spirit. Hendriksen expresses it:

> Paul prays that in the hearts and lives of the Philippians there may be a rich spiritual harvest, consisting of a multitude of the fairest fruits of heaven; such as, love, joy, peace, longsuffering, kindness, goodness, faithfulness, gentleness, self-control (Gal. 5:22, 23), and the works which result from these dispositions. One of these works, a very important one, is soul-winning (Prov. 11:30).[13]

What Paul is seeking to be fulfilled in their lives is not something which is a product of human effort or legalism, nor is it advanced by the Judaizing party in Rome referred to in Philippians 1:15, or by any other natural source. It must be a supernatural work of grace in answer to prayer.

The ultimate goal of his prayer is not only transformation of the Philippians, but through this to bring glory and praise to God. The thought is not that God will praise them, but rather that the Philippians will be an occasion of manifesting God's glory and of bringing praise to the Lord. The depths of Paul's concern and love for the Philippians, and the high standard of conduct and experience here described, succinctly express the true goals in life for any Christian. Love with discernment and perception, distinguishing the good from the bad, sincerity of motive and purity of life, and abundance of the fruits of righteousness produced by the grace of God are the hallmarks of spiritual attainment, both for the Philippians and for us.

In this introductory section to the epistle, Paul has under-✳ scored two important aspects of Christian faith and life. The first is the assurance of salvation, and the certainty of glorification based on the grace of God and the finished work of Christ, although manifested experientially by a contemporary work of grace in the lives of Christians. The apostle is, first of all, rejoicing in the salvation of the Philippian Christians. Second, satisfied as to their supernatural salvation, he is burdened that now they will go on to achieve the full fruit of the Christian life and the fruit of the Spirit, including love, joy, holiness, and service. They had attained much, but there was still more to be realized in their Christian faith.

PAUL'S IMPRISONMENT AS AN AID TO PROCLAMATION OF THE GOSPEL, 1:12-18

The experience of Paul of suffering in prison gives remarkable insight into the purposes of God in permitting the affliction of His children. As is so often the case, "Surely the wrath of man shall praise thee" (Ps 76:10). What appears on the surface a great tragedy—an effective preacher and missionary rendered immobile for years in the most fruitful period of his life—turns out to be an effective platform of personal witness in Rome and a time for quiet meditation which permitted the writing of the precious prison epistles which, with the epistle to the Romans, are the heart of Paul's revelation to the church.

To the Philippian Christians, grieving at Paul's confinement, the purpose of God in Paul's suffering is revealed as he says, "The things which happened unto me have fallen out rather unto the furtherance of the gospel" (v. 12). Instead of hindering the proclamation of the gospel, his circumstances had served to extend his witness and to testify to his triumph over suffering.

The problem of human suffering is one of the most profound theological and philosophic questions to confront intelligent minds. If there is a God, why does He permit suffering? And if He is a God of love, why in particular does He permit those who trust Him to suffer? The extent of human suffering in the world in the form of physical want—such as lack of food and clothing, the anxiety and fear of those who live in superstition or political oppression, and the intellectual suffering coming from the normal stresses and strains of life—are all beyond human calculation. Although many solutions have been offered, the Christian faith is the only comprehensive answer.

According to the Scriptures, suffering is caused by the fact of sin and a disordered world. Much suffering in the world is the natural consequence of the disobedience of Adam and Eve and the resulting sinfulness of the race. Sin has come by the will of man in his rebellion against God rather than by an act of God. It is understandable that a righteous God will need to judge sinful man. But obviously Paul is not suffering because he is a sinner.

How is human suffering explained as it relates to the child of God? Why should one like Paul, who has been saved by grace and whose sins have been forgiven and who has served God acceptably, be placed in such a situation as Paul was experiencing in prison? The answer is given in various portions of Paul's own epistles, and at least four major reasons can be enumerated to explain why Christians suffer:

First, suffering may come in the life of a believer because of failure to judge sin in his life. Paul refers to this in 1 Corinthians 11:31-32 where he writes, after calling attention to God's judgment on the Corinthians, "For if we would judge ourselves, we should not be judged. But when we are judged, we are chastened of the Lord, that we should not be condemned with the world." In other words, the Corinthian church had experienced physical weakness and even death because of their failure to judge their own sins. This, however, does not seem to be Paul's difficulty.

Second, another reason for suffering is mentioned by Paul in Romans 5:3-5, which presents suffering as a means of gaining spiritual experience. Paul wrote there, "And not only so, but we glory in tribulations also: knowing that tribulation worketh patience; and patience, experience; and experience, hope; and hope maketh not ashamed; because the love of God is shed abroad in our hearts by the Holy Ghost which is given unto us." An outstanding illustration of this is the case in the Old Testament of Job who is described as a perfect and righteous man but nevertheless permitted to suffer, that through his suffering he might learn more of the nature of God and His dealings with man.

Third, still another cause for suffering is that it is a device used by God to prevent sin in the life of a Christian. To this Paul alludes in 2 Corinthians where he stated his own experience of a thorn in the flesh:

> And lest I should be exalted above measure through the abundance of the revelations, there was given to me a thorn in the flesh, the messenger of Satan to buffet me, lest I should be exalted above measure. For this thing I besought the Lord thrice, that it might depart from me. And he said unto me, My grace is sufficient for thee: for my strength is made perfect in weakness. Most gladly therefore will I rather glory in my infirmities, that the power of Christ may rest upon me (2 Co 12:7-9).

There is no evidence that Paul was imprisoned to keep him

from sinning, however, and his imprisonment was not his thorn in the flesh.

Fourth, an important reason for suffering is to increase the effectiveness of a Christian's testimony. This seems to be the best explanation why Paul was in prison. God had used this peculiar circumstance to give him a means of presenting many with the gospel who otherwise would have been beyond Paul's reach. Athough he does not mention all the details, Paul states that because of his bonds in Christ, referring to the fact that he was chained constantly to a Roman soldier, the gospel by this means had been manifested "in all the palace, and in all other places."

The translation "in all the palace" (v. 13) is literally "in all the praetorian." As explained in the Introduction, the praetorium can refer to a palace or the place of residence of the governor (cf. Mt 27:27; Mk 15:16; Ac 23:35). This is the way it is rendered in the Authorized Version. There are, however, other possibilities, such as referring to the barracks or camp of the praetorian guards. A third possibility is that it refers to the guards themselves because the phrase is immediately followed with "and in all other places," or more literally, "and to all the rest." It has been argued by Lightfoot and many others that the best rendering is to consider the reference to the soldiers themselves, and accordingly is translated, "throughout the praetorian guard," which Lightfoot says is "the best supported meaning."[14] If so, it supports the idea that Paul was in Rome. If it refers to a palace or a government house, it is argued that it might refer to a place other than Rome, such as Ephesus. The majority opinion supports Lightfoot; although, as pointed out in the Introduction, some have preferred one of the other renderings which would permit the letter to be written from Ephesus or some other place. If the majority opinion is followed, however, Paul was guarded by imperial soldiers who were the cream of the Roman army, and the time of his writing was while he was in Rome, the center of the Roman government.

Whether in Rome or elsewhere, however, according to the custom, the apostle was probably chained to a Roman soldier twenty-four hours a day, with a new guard every six hours. No doubt this was a most trying experience which subjected Paul to all the evil characteristics and whims of his guard even when he talked to his friends, when he prayed or when he attempted to write. Always there was this Roman guard.

The circumstances, however, also afforded him the priceless opportunity of witness, and each guard heard Paul's story. The claims of the grace of God and the transformation it afforded in his life subjected him to the scrutiny of each guard to see whether his testimony was genuine. The slightest deviation, impatience, or irritation would disqualify his testimony to the guard, and any lack of consistency in life would soon be communicated to others. The apostle's sincerity and his glowing account of God's grace manifested to him apparently were effective as guard after guard came to know Jesus Christ in an effective way.

Only God knows what went on in the rented room in which Paul was permitted to live. There the guards heard the conversation of Paul with his intimate friends and were able to ask questions about the strange words which they heard from their prisoner. In the lonely hours of the dark night, illuminated only by the moon, many a guard probably heard the testimony of Paul—his early career as a Pharisee, his antagonism and persecution of Christians, his remarkable conversion, and the causes of his imprisonment. No doubt all this was the subject of much conversation in the prae-

torian guard, and raised sympathy among the soldiers as
they understood his unjust imprisonment. His chains had
become an effective line of communication to the elite soldiers of the Roman Empire who, if converted, could carry
the gospel to the ends of the earth as they were moved from
place to place. It reminds us that every circumstance of life
is a platform on which the transforming grace of God can
be manifested in the life of the Lord's own.

Paul's testimony was not limited to the guards, but was
manifest "in all other places," literally, "to all the rest," that
is, to other persons. What Paul said and did in that prison
were apparently discussed, especially among the Jews who
lived at Rome. These brethren of Paul in the flesh were very
conscious, not only that Paul was a Jew, but that he was
accused by his fellow Jews of breaking with the tradition
of the fathers. Paul's prison had become a pulpit.

One effect of Paul's faithful and consistent witness was
that "many," literally, "the greater number" of the brethren
in the Lord were made more bold to speak the Word without
fear. If Paul could preach in prison fearlessly, they could
preach the Word outside prison. His influence was such that
the great majority of Christians in Rome were encouraged to
witness.

There were, however, two factions among Christians in
Rome. One group loved and followed Paul. The other group
were the Judaizers (3:1-6) who held onto their Jewish traditions. Although they believed in Christ, they attempted to
combine Judaism and Christianity. The inference that Paul's
opponents were Judaizers, derived from his condemnation
of them in 3:1-6, seems to be justified. Lightfoot, for instance, states,

> These antagonists can be none other than the Judaizing
> party, who call down the Apostle's rebuke in a later passage

of this letter (iii. 2. sq.), and whose opposition is indirectly implied in another epistle written also from Rome (Col. iv. 11); see above pp. 17, 18.[15]

Ignoring the contribution of Philippians 3, Muller opposes this view, saying,

> The idea, that Paul here has in mind the Judaizers, (so among others Bengal, Lightfoot, Meyer, Ellicott), must be rejected, for in these verses no *material* contrast is mentioned between their preaching and that of Paul, but only a *personal* one. Thrice the apostle pertinently declares that they preach Christ (15, 17, 18).[16]

Note, however, that Muller is arguing entirely from silence, and that it is not impossible for a Judaizer to preach Christ. It may be that the degree of their error was not as serious as in the Galatian churches, but there must have been something more than a personal antagonism to Paul.

Paul's message seems to have been too revolutionary for them. In contending for their point of view, however, they did preach Christ; and hence Paul refers to them as motivated by "envy and strife" (v. 15) and as preaching "Christ of contention, not sincerely, supposing to add affliction to my bonds" (v. 16). They probably regarded Paul's imprisonment as an act of divine chastening. Others, inspired by Paul, defended the gospel of grace motivated by love of God and love of Paul.

Although Paul ardently defends the gospel of grace in the epistle to the Galatians, he concludes here that even if they preached with wrong motivation, "Christ is preached; and I therein do rejoice, yea, and will rejoice" (v. 18). As Lightfoot points out, this is not a repudiation of the gospel of grace which he so vigorously defends in Galatians, nor is it a condoning of the Judaizing party. As Lightfoot puts it,

> Here on the other hand the choice is between an imper-
> fect Christianity and an unconverted state; the former,
> however inadequate, must be a gain upon the latter, there-
> fore must give joy to a high-minded servant of Christ. In
> Rome there was room enough for him and for them.[17]

The greatest problem of the world then and now is not
that the gospel is imperfectly preached, but that it is not
preached at all. Instead of adding affliction to his chains, it
brought joy to Paul that his presence in Rome had served
to extend the preaching of the gospel.

Paul's entire experience recognized the wisdom of God
in permitting Paul to suffer. Divine revelation offers the only
satisfactory explanation as to why there is suffering in the
world as a whole, and why even the godly suffer. Paul was
in prison as a means of increasing his testimony, as an effective way to evangelize Rome, and to prepare him spiritually
to write the prison epistles.

Although the reasons for suffering may not always be
immediately apparent, by faith a Christian can assume "that
all things work together for good to them that love God"
(Ro 8:28). Many a great Christian was molded in character in the crucible of suffering, matured in loneliness, and
prepared for greater usefulness in God's hands than if untouched by the storms of life.

PAUL'S SUFFERING AS AN AID TO MAGNIFICATION
OF CHRIST, 1:19-20

Although it would be natural for Paul to consider the antagonism of the Judaizers as another aspect of his affliction,
he rejoices in it, not only because it furthered the gospel, but
because it stimulated prayer on the part of his friends. His
circumstances being what they were, he expresses confidence
that because of their prayers and "the supply of the Spirit

of Jesus Christ" (v. 19) literally, "the bountiful supply," he will experience salvation. By this he means God's total deliverance, not only spiritual but from the prison. The Spirit of God is both the one supplied and the Supplier of Paul's needs, both the Giver and the Gift (cf. Ro 8:9; Gal 4:6; and Ac 16:7, ASV).[18]

This living hope of the apostle leads to the reaffirmation of his supreme goal in life—to magnify or glorify Christ. He believes his future deliverance will be "according to my earnest expectation and my hope"; that his experience of deliverance and effective witness will leave him with nothing of which to be ashamed. Whether by life or death, he wants his witness to be so bold that Christ will be magnified in his body.

Paul expresses this fervently but delicately. He does not use the first person or say, "I will glorify Christ," but rather selects the future passive. The thought is not that the glory of Christ will be increased, but rather that it will be manifested and made apparent to others. This was his passion as hour by hour he bore witness to the guard at his side, and this was to be his testimony even to his tormentors, the Judaizers. His utter committal to this goal is indicated by his willingness to achieve it whether "by life, or by death."

Paul was not concerned as to how he would become the magnifying glass which would enable others of dim spiritual sight to see the glories of Christ. Sufficient for him was the thought that he could be the medium. Such has always been the true goal of the spiritually great. John the Baptist had said, "He must increase, but I must decrease" (Jn 3:30). As Guy King has noted, an object can be magnified by the microscope, making the little big, or the telescope, making that afar off to be seen as if very near.[19]

To Live or to Die, 1:21-24

Paul's willingness to die if necessary for Christ was not necessarily an evil alternative. In the memorable statement of verse 21, in many respects the key verse of the epistle, he states the alternatives. For to Paul to live is Christ. By this he means that his life is wrapped up in Christ, in witnessing of Christ, in fellowship with Christ, in the goal to make his life a channel through which others might know Christ. For others, life may be different. As F. B. Meyer observes, life for the merchant may be wealth; for the slave, toil and suffering; for the philosopher, knowledge; for the soldier, fame; for the emperor, an empire.[20]

But to die is not to give up Christ, but rather it is to gain. To die would be freedom from the chains, deliverance from self, the end of suffering, the curtain on strife, the beginning of a new life of freedom and abundance, the experience of being completely like Christ. The alternate claims of life and the glorious prospect of life after death conflict sharply in the mind of Paul. If he continues to live in the flesh, there would be fruit for his labor. There is obviously an ellipsis in thought. Probably he did not question whether to continue living would have produced fruit. There seems to have been assurance that he would live on. His thought is simple: If I do live on and produce fruit, would this be better than to die? Paul finds himself torn between the alternatives, perhaps preferring, if left to his own wishes, "to depart, and to be with Christ; which is far better" (v. 23).

He recognizes, however, that if he remains in the flesh he can help others such as the Philippians (v. 24). The expressions in the original are perhaps more graphic than their English translation. He describes his conflict as being in "a strait," a verb meaning "to be held close"; hence, "to be distressed" or "tormented," "pressed from every side." The word "depart" means to "loose" or "untie." Literally it means "to break up," as to break up camp as Israel did in the wilderness. The departure from earth to heaven is indeed breaking earthly ties and moving camp to heaven. But the tug of ties binding him to the earth and the need of those left behind make departure difficult.

Assurance of His Coming Acquittal, 1:25-26

Having come to the conclusion that his continued life and ministry on earth are more needful than to depart to be with Christ, he proceeds confidently to assert his assurance of his acquittal at his coming trial, which would permit him to continue his ministry to the Philippians and others. In other words, because staying would be more helpful than going to heaven, Paul is assured of his release and his continual ministry.

Accordingly, he says, "I know that I shall abide and continue with you all for your furtherance and joy of faith" (v. 25). This is not so much prophetic insight as human judgment; but, according to 1 Timothy 1:3, he fulfilled his purpose to revisit Macedonia. His renewed fellowship with them would contribute to the furtherance or progress of their faith, as well as their joy. This in turn would result in their rejoicing more abundantly in Christ, literally, "boasting," because of answered prayer in bringing Paul back to them again. This was to be fulfilled in the brief period between his release from his first trial and his second trial and execution. At this time neither the apostle nor the Philippians realized how short the respite would be, and how near the time of his departure when the executioner's ax would flash for one brief moment outside the gates of Rome. Yet now, as in the last moments of his life, he could declare, "The

Lord shall deliver me from every evil work, and will preserve me unto his heavenly kingdom" (2 Ti 4:18).

Although the common belief that Paul was released from his first imprisonment has been challenged, there is considerable evidence that he fulfilled a fourth missionary journey which included a trip to Spain before the increased persecution under Nero broke out. References to a visit to Crete (Titus 1:5), the winter in Nicopolis (Titus 3:12), the trip to Macedonia which is not mentioned in Acts (1 Ti 1:3), the visit to Troas and Miletus (2 Ti 4:13-20), all support this view. The early church Fathers such as Eusebius, Clement of Rome, Chrysostom, and Hieronymus, interpreted the Scriptures as supporting the two imprisonments.[21]

EXHORTATION TO UNITY, FEARLESSNESS AND STEADFASTNESS, 1:27-30

In view of the possibility of Paul's visiting them soon or, in any event, hearing tidings of how they were getting along, he exhorts them, "Only let your conversation be as it becometh the gospel of Christ" (v. 27). The verb literally means "to perform their duty as a good citizen." That is, they were to be good citizens of God's kingdom, and to act in a manner becoming those who have believed in the gospel of Christ.

The use of a political metaphor to illustrate spiritual truth comes out of the context that Philippi was a Roman colony where a Roman citizen such as Paul would be very conscious of civil responsibility. Paul uses the same metaphor in Philippians 3:20 and Ephesians 2:19. Although Paul repeatedly was accused of violating Roman laws, actually he was subject to the higher law of the kingdom of God. He wanted the Philippians to likewise be good citizens of the heavenly kingdom. Although the Philippian church was independent, they respected Paul's apostolic office and wanted his approbation. Paul is stating in effect that he will sooner or later review the state of the church, especially in the matter of their unity. In keeping with the current problem in the church, he exhorts them to "stand fast in one spirit, with one mind striving together for the faith of the gospel."

In his exhortation to unity, standing fast "in one spirit," he is probably using "spirit" in an impersonal sense rather than in reference to the Holy Spirit. They should have a unity of principle, attitude and motivation. This, of course, would come from the guidance of the Holy Spirit. The expression "one mind" is the translation of a word meaning "soul" or "life."[22] It is the root of the English word *psychology* and, therefore, refers to the whole experiential aspect of man. In a word, Paul is appealing to unity in principle as well as action. Even the word for "striving" has a prefix translated "together" and, therefore, refers to united action. Although the Christian should be independent of the world, he should be dependent and guided by the Spirit of God in the united action with those of like mind. Conflicts within the church originate in human failure, not diversity of divine principle or guidance.

But all the problem was not within the church. They also had adversaries without, as Paul himself was experiencing. The adversaries—literally, "those standing against them," from the word for "lying" or "standing," plus *anti* or *against* —no doubt threatened persecution of the Philippian church. Paul exhorts them not to be intimidated. Although persecution and trial as they come into the life of a Christian may be interpreted by the unbelieving world as the disfavor of God —evidence that they are under God's judgment—they are actually just the opposite—evidence that they are separated from the world that knows not salvation and knows not God. Their fearlessness was a token also of the certainty of their deliverance of God and of ultimate judgment on their adversaries.[23] As early Christians were thrown to the lions and tortured in many hideous ways, it may have seemed to the unbelieving world that they were forsaken of God. The very hatred of Satan and the extent of their suffering demonstrated that they shared suffering with Christ and Paul, which is naturally the lot of those who run counter to this world. Rather than avoid the suffering by compromise, Paul exhorts them to be willing not only to believe in Christ but to bear the suffering which often goes with it. Being in prison himself, he was able to say, "Having the same conflict which ye saw in me, and now hear to be in me" (v.30).

In mentioning his own suffering, he was not only referring to his present imprisonment but to the suffering which the Philippians themselves had observed in the founding of the church in Acts 16. Paul was no disassociated observer of what it means to suffer for Christ and was in a good position to exhort them to be like-minded. Paul's decision that he would prefer to continue living was undoubtedly motivated by his desire to help the Philippian church. In verses 26-29 four reasons are itemized:

First, that by his coming again to the Philippian church, their "rejoicing may be more abundant in Jesus Christ" (v. 26). Second, the prospect that he might visit them or, in any case, hear of their affairs, would tend to encourage them to Christian unity, to "stand fast in one spirit, with one mind striving together for the faith of the gospel" (v. 27). Third, his deliverance from prison, and faithfulness in suffering would encourage them to be fearless in their own proclamation of the gospel so that they would not be terrified by their adversaries (v. 28). Fourth, having observed Paul's faithfulness in suffering, they would be willing also to suffer for Christ's sake (vv. 29-30).

Chapter 1 as a whole sets the stage for the exhortations and revelations which were to follow. His evident love for the Philippians, his confidence in God's grace, and his earnest desire that they might attain to the utmost the fruits of righteousness which belong to the Christian faith all provided a platform on which he could exhort them to remedy what seems to be their only major failure—a lack of close fellowship and unity. Having already referred to his own testimony in suffering, in the next chapter he introduces three additional outstanding illustrations of those completely dedicated to the will of God—Jesus Christ, Timothy, and Epaphroditus. In it he demonstrates that unity is a by-product of walking with God.

This great introductory chapter to this epistle provides so much by way of revelation, inspiration and exhortation. The portrait it affords of the apostle Paul is in itself an example to all believers and one which should bring comfort and reassurance to those suffering for Christ's sake. The note of joy and thanksgiving, a testimony to his triumph over suffering, is prominent in the chapter, and is as a ray of sunlight in the midst of shadows. The dominant place of love in Christian relationship permeates the entire chapter and prepares the way for Paul's further exhortation to unity in the Philippian church. Paul's example and practice of prayer is a means of spiritual progress, and his earnest concern for the spiritual welfare of others is an exhortation for all to follow. His confidence in the will of God in the ultimate outworking for good, his triumph over suffering, and his earnest and supreme desire in all things—whether living or dying—to glorify Christ, provide the motivating principles which enable him to exhort the Philippians to unity, courage, and steadfastness. How much has been communicated in comparatively few words, and how rich its content and inspiration.

2

TRIUMPH IN SERVICE

THE FELLOWSHIP OF CHRISTIAN LOVE, 2:1-4

HAVING ALLUDED to Christian unity several times in chapter 1, the apostle in chapter 2 now presents in a formal way the full argument for unity of mind and heart, elements so essential to any triumph in Christian service. The main principles are expounded in verses 1-4. The supreme example is Christ, presented in the classic passage which portrays His humiliation, obedience unto death, and exaltation. The chapter closes with three additional illustrations—Paul himself, Timothy, and Epaphroditus—all pointed examples of those who triumphed in their service for God.

While this chapter is, therefore, primarily exhortation and inspiration, it contains also the greatest statement theologically of what Christ did when He became man, died, and rose again. While affirming His humiliation and death, it presents Him also as the Son of God before whom every knee shall bow. In many respects chapter 2 is the high point in the epistle.

In the opening four verses in which the appeal for spiritual unity is presented, the fourfold "if" of verse 1 in the English translation unduly emphasizes the conditions governing the exhortation, as if the outcome was uncertain. More accurately translated, the word *because* could be substituted. It is *because* of the realities of God's grace, common to all

Christians, that Christians should be of one mind. The
reference to "consolation in Christ" is probably better translated "exhortation," as Lightfoot suggests.[1] Not only is there
encouragement, but there is the comfort of love, another
word primarily meaning "encouragement" and hence "consolation."[2] Both of the first two factors deal with motivation
(cf. similar use of the words in 1 Th 2:11).

The third argument for spiritual unity is the fellowship of
the Spirit (cf. 2 Co 13:14, "the communion of the Holy
Ghost"). Although "Spirit" does not have the article, and
grammatically could refer to the communion of human
spirits, that is, ordinary human fellowship, translators have
almost universally regarded this as a reference to the Holy
Spirit who is causal factor in spiritual unity.

The fourth and final reason for spiritual unity is based on
the appeal to "bowels and mercies," paraphrased by Lightfoot as "any affectionate yearnings of heart, any tender feelings of compassion."[3] The ancients regarded the seat of
emotions in the bowels much as in modern times emotion
is related to the heart. A feeling of compassion experientially
seems to grip the entire body and is not purely an intellectual decision. Spiritual unity, then, depends also upon the
emotional heart of man moved by the Spirit of God. A
Christian who is exhorted by Christ, encouraged by the
knowledge of His love, experiencing fellowship of the Holy
Spirit, and possessing a true heart of compassion and attitude of mercy is equipped to realize spiritual unity.

Paul exhorts them, however, on the basis of bringing joy
to his heart, "fulfill ye my joy" (v. 2). The thought is to
"fill full" or "complete" his cup of joy, already almost run-
ning over, by their many manifestations of love toward him.
This could be accomplished by being "likeminded," that is,
having the same mind, "having the same love," the *agape*[4]

of God, "being of one accord," literally, "one-souled," and "of one mind," similar but a stronger statement than of being "likeminded." In his zeal to communicate to the Philippians the spiritual unity which he longs to see manifested in them, the apostle piles up descriptive words which somewhat overlap, and yet each contributes to the total picture.

In verse 3 he deals with the practical outworking of spiritual unity. Christians who are really one in Christ and in fellowship one with the other will do nothing in the spirit of "strife" which would produce factions, or through "vainglory," that which would glorify themselves and increase their vanity. Instead of operating selfishly and without regard to fellowship with others, motivated by pride, they should manifest "lowliness of mind," godly humility which tends to magnify the virtues of others. It is interesting that the Greek word translated "lowliness of mind"—the ordinary word for "mind" with the adjective "low" added, a common word in the New Testament—does not occur in Greek literature until the writing of the New Testament. It was distinctively a Christian grace. True humility breaks down the barriers of envy, jealousy, and suspicion of self-interest.

In verse 4 the added virtue of unselfishness, abandoning self-interest, and looking out for the welfare of others, is the natural fruit of the spiritual unity he is urging.

The first four verses of this chapter are, as F. B. Meyer expresses it, "the entwining of Christian hearts."[5] Although ecumenicity organizationally, that is, a world church, is not exhorted in the Bible, ecumenicity spiritually is. Within the local church as well as within the body of Christ generally, there should be true spiritual unity and no schism of fellowship. This is the normal expression of love which Christ offered as the supreme badge of discipleship (Jn 13:35).

The Humiliation of Christ as Our Example,
2:5-8

In support of the exhortation of the first four verses of this chapter, Paul now introduces Jesus Christ as the supreme illustration of compassion, self-abnegation, and humility. The act of incarnation in which God became man, the humble circumstances and sufferings of Christ in life, and the supreme act of dying on the cross establish Jesus Christ as the greatest illustration of one completely unselfish and entirely devoted to others.

Although presented as an exhortation, the passage is most important theologically as defining what is called the *kenosis*. This word is derived from the Greek word *ekenosen,* meaning *to empty*. In becoming man, how did this act of humiliation affect His deity, and of what did He empty Himself? A careful examination of this passage will reveal that Christ retained His complete deity, but restricted its manifestation and did not use His divine powers for His own benefit.

Paul begins with the exhortation, "Let this mind be in you, which was also in Christ Jesus" (v. 5). By "mind" he means literally that we should think within ourselves, or in our hearts, just as Christ did when He became incarnate. The expression in the original is somewhat unusual, but the meaning is clear. Our thinking, our attitude, our opinion, our evaluation of the situation which faces us should be the same as Christ's when He faced His supreme act of humiliation and death.

In brief, we should think Christ's thoughts. If our situation is such that under certain circumstances we might be tempted to promote our self-interest, defend our own rights, and assert our own virtues, how much more would this be true of Christ? How great, therefore, is His humility. Christ, in spite of His divine attributes, His eternal glory, and His rightful claim to worship and obedience, willingly put aside the insignia of divinity and put on the robes of humanity.

A series of descriptive phrases is used to define this supreme act. First, it is stated that Christ was "in the form of God." The word "form" (Gk, *morphe*) indicates external manifestation, but it is more than mere appearance or a disguise. The form is in keeping with His real essence or being. Although a dictionary definition of *morphe* would be "form, outward appearance, shape, gener. a bodily form,"[6] the usage of the word theologically, as William Hendriksen points out, makes it refer "to the inner, essential and abiding nature of a person or thing."[7]

This is brought out in such passages as Romans 8:29, 2 Corinthians 3:18, and Galatians 4:19, where the "form" or being "conformed" refers not to the outer but the inner nature. Its meaning, therefore, is in contrast to "fashion," referring to outer appearance mentioned in verse 8.[8] Being in the form of God states, then, that externally, in eternity past, He had manifested what He really is—the eternal God. The word translated "being" means prior existence. Although it is a different word than the verb *to be* which would directly affirm eternal existence, theologically it is tantamount to affirming His eternal existence. The point here is merely that before He became man He had the form of God.

In the incarnation, however, Christ by becoming man "thought it not robbery to be equal with God"; that is, He did not hold the outer manifestation of His deity as a treasure that had to be grasped and retained. The original represents it as a prize or a treasure which could be stolen, and therefore requiring effort to retain and protect. Christ in His incarnation did not concern Himself with retaining the outer manifestation of deity which He had prior to His birth. Hence, verse 6 can be translated, ¡Who, being in the form of God, completely manifesting His divine nature, did not consider the display of His attributes demonstrating that He is equal with God, something to be held onto as a rich prize." In becoming man, Christ, therefore, divested Himself of the outward appearance of deity while retaining all the attributes that belong to God.

This is summarized in the expression, "but made himself of no reputation" (v. 7); literally, "He emptied Himself" in that He became obedient unto death. The Greek word *ekenosen,* which means *to empty,* is a dramatic way of expressing the tremendous change in the outer appearance of Christ which took place in the incarnation. Lightfoot defines *ekenosen* as " 'emptied,* stripped *Himself'* of the insignia of majesty."[9] Some have attempted to argue from this that Christ gave up His deity or some of His divine attributes. What is meant, however, must be defined by the explanation which accompanies this statement, namely, that Christ did not empty Himself of His deity, but only of its outward manifestation and its use for His own benefit.

The extent of the *kenosis* or the self-emptying of Christ is embodied in four expressions in this passage. The first, already considered, indicates that He superimposed upon the form of deity the form of a servant (v. 7), becoming, literally, a slave. The act of "emptying" Himself and assuming the form of a slave was one act and was a part of His incarnation. It is significant that the Scriptures, while declaring that Christ emptied Himself, do not state that He gave up the form of deity. It is obvious that He gave up the outer manifestation of deity, but the act of assuming humanity and the form of a servant was superimposed upon His deity without taking away His divine attributes. He was like a king who temporarily puts on the garments of a peasant while at the same time remaining king, even though it was not outwardly apparent. Christ could not have achieved His earthly purpose if He had manifested the effulgent glory which He had from eternity past. He needed to *appear* as a man, even if He still were God.

Second, He "was made in the likeness of man." The word "likeness" (Gk, *homoiomati*) means that Christ was like other men, had the essential attributes of humanity, and manifested these in living among men as a genuine man. It is significant that in referring to being "made in the likeness of men" (v. 7), the plural for "men" is used. As Lightfoot explains, "For Christ, as the second Adam, represents not the individual man, but the human race; Rom. v.15, I Cor. xv.45-47."[10] This, of course, means that Christ had all the qualities which Adam as a genuine man had before Adam sinned, but not the sin nature which came through Adam's failure. In a word, He was a genuine man having a soul, spirit and body, and, in this sense, was one of the human race.

Third, He was "found in fashion as a man" (v. 8). The word "fashion" is from the Greek work *schemati* which refers to outer manifestation and the more transient characteristics of humanity. He wore the clothes and acted like men of His generation. The thought in the Greek word *schemati* is that "fashion" can change while the *morphe* does not. Hence in 1 Corinthians 7:31 it is stated, "The fashion of this world passeth away." Satan in 2 Corinthians 11:14 puts on the outer garb of an angel. Christians are exhorted in 1 Peter 1:14, "As obedient children, not fashioning yourselves according to the former lusts in your ignorance." In Romans 12:2 the two words *schema* and *morphe* are brought together, and the Christian is instructed not to "fashion" himself after the world, but to be "transformed," changed in his inner nature and experience.[11] Although His humanity was to continue forever, Christ's outer fashion was to be changed when He resumed His place in glory.

The three Greek words *morphe* (form), *homoiomati* (likeness), and *schemati* (fashioned) state on the one hand that Christ was still all that God is after He became incarnate; but that, on the other hand, He had a genuine humanity, manifested in being in form as a servant, like other men except that He was not a sinner, and in outer appearance or fashion looked like a man and acted like a man. The fact is that while Christ was man on earth, He still was man after His resurrection and is still a man in glory. While on earth He was God and looked like a man; in glory, while He will retain His humanity, He will resume the appearance of God and His prerogatives of deity.

Having stated the dramatic change in the person of Christ when He took upon Himself a complete humanity, Paul in verse 8 describes what Christ did in His new human state. Not only did He condescend to become a man, in the form of a slave, and in the likeness of man, but He suffered complete humiliation, voluntarily being willing to die, expressed in the clause "became obedient unto death." Then the apostle adds, "even the death of the cross." Here was the eternal Son of God, all that God is, becoming man but going beyond anything that God required of man, that is, to be obedient to the death of the cross with its unspeakable physical and spiritual suffering described in Psalm 22. This humiliation is dramatically presented prophetically in Isaiah 53, a chapter which a student of Philippians 2 should read thoughtfully and prayerfully. In Isaiah the glorious coming King is described prophetically in His first coming as having "no form nor comeliness," with "no beauty that we should desire him," one "despised and rejected of men," one who was to be "wounded for our transgressions," and "bruised for our iniquities" (Is 53:2-5).

Ordinary men have been humiliated and have died violent, painful deaths, but never did one die as Christ died. He had it in His power to come down from the cross and destroy His enemies, and yet He willingly died, not only suffering the unspeakable agony, but the torture of soul of a holy person bearing the sins of the whole world and for the first time experiencing separation from God the Father. No human frame has ever entered into the experience of Christ, the obedient Servant, who coming from the infinite height of glory went to the infinite depth of hell. John Calvin pointed out, "For by dying in this manner He was not only covered with ignominy in the sight of God, but was also accursed in the sight of God."[12]

How little our sacrifices, our acts of unselfishness, and our suffering the slights of men seem in the shadow of that cross. If Christ was willing to do this for us, what stands in the way of our forgiving others and having complete spiritual fellowship with all those of like mind in Christ? This eloquent portrayal of the example of Christ as triumphant in His work and service must have had a telling effect upon the Philippian church and should today cut through the pride and foolish self-interest which often keeps Christians from having the mind of Christ.

THE EXALTATION AND GLORIFICATION OF CHRIST,
2:9-11

But the cross was not the end but the entrance into glory! Although Paul does not make the application, the implication is that those who share Christ's suffering will also share His glory. Calvin expressed it, "By adding consolation, He shews that abasement, to which the human mind is averse,

is in the highest degree desirable. . . . Every one therefore
that humbles himself will in like manner be exalted."[13] The
body that was laid in the tomb in the garden, was raised in
resurrection power and ascended into heaven where its glory
was completely revealed.

The exaltation which Christ experienced when He went
to heaven (v. 9) was not only the resumption of the glory
which He had before the incarnation [1](Jn 17:5), but the
added glory of triumph over sin, suffering and death, and
the fulfillment of God that in His death He would reconcile
the world unto Himself (2 Co 5:19). It was in recognition
of this achievement that He is given "a name which is above
every name . . . the name of Jesus."

It is significant that although the three primary names
for God designate the same Person, that the name Jesus—the
human name that means Saviour—should be used as the
exalted name instead of Lord, which refers to His sovereignty and deity. Christ refers to His being anointed the
Messiah of Israel and Prophet, Priest and King by the Holy
Spirit. Although it is true, as Lightfoot points out, that the
name Jesus may be construed in the genitive, that is, "the
name *of* Jesus," the dative is spelled exactly the same way,
and it could be translated "the name Jesus." In any case, it
is the one bearing the human name that is divinely exalted.[14]
It was the name of Jesus that summed up both His humiliation and triumph, for only as the God-Man who would die
on the cross could He be the Saviour.

Not only is the name of Jesus above every name, that is,
above all others whose names might indicate greatness; but
the name of Jesus is the name of the Person who is supremely
sovereign, before whom all creatures must bow. The term
"the name" means not simply a title given, but all that the
title represents by way of office, attainment, rank, or dignity.

Hence "the name" of God includes all that the majesty of God represents. The point is that the same Person who suffered humiliation and crucifixion becomes, not only by means of His person but by means of His triumph, the one to whom all must bow.

This statement, patterned after Isaiah 45:23, which is directly quoted in Romans 14:11, indicates the extent of the ultimate triumph of Christ. The bowed knee will acknowledge His lordship, deity, and sovereignty. The comprehensive statement of those who will bow at the name of Jesus includes all creation. This certainly would involve all classes of men and angels. Lightfoot goes beyond this to suggest that all of nature is in view in the same sense that Paul represents all creation in Romans 8:22 as awaiting the redemption of Christ.[15] Muller is probably right when he objects to Lightfoot's position, which would include all nature, in that it can hardly be conceived that inanimate nature could bend a knee and with a tongue make confession.[16] Probably, as Muller suggests, the three classifications are (1) heavenly beings (angels and the whole world of immaterial spirits), (2) inhabitants (people living on earth at the time), and (3) those under the earth (those who have descended into hades, that is, lost souls who have not gone to heaven).[17] While it is true that the three adjectives referring to heaven, earth and under the earth could be interpreted as neuter, that is, inanimate creation; they could also be taken as masculine, that is, the creatures in these areas.

Not only will every knee bow, but "Every tongue should confess that Jesus Christ is Lord, to the glory of God the Father" (v. 11). Here are all three primary names for Christ. While it remains remarkable that verse 10 uses only the name Jesus, which is the human name meaning Saviour, it is clear that His person includes all that the primary names represent. Every tongue, therefore, is obligated to confess that Jesus the Saviour, who is also the Christ and the anointed of the Holy Spirit, is Lord, that is, sovereign God. This should be done to the glory of God the Father, for it is the Father's purpose that His Son should be glorified.

As translated in the Authorized Version, the verb is "should confess," that is, merely stating that the situation is such, and the Person is such that every tongue *ought* to confess Jesus Christ as Lord. This is based on the translation of a Greek word *exomologesetai* which is in the aorist subjunctive and is the reading found in two texts known as *Aleph* and *B*. An alternate reading achieved by changing just one letter makes the word future indicative, hence to be translated, "shall confess" instead of "should confess," and is supported by a number of ancient Greek manuscripts (*A C D F G K L P*).[18] The future tense is indicated in the quotation of Isaiah 45:23. Of course, it is true that every knee *should* bow and every tongue *should* confess, but it is also true that they *shall* bow, and this is stated in Romans 14:11.

This leads to the conclusion that all men, whether righteous or unrighteous, and all angels, whether holy or fallen, will some day be forced to confess and bow before the Lord Jesus Christ. The sad fact is, however, that that reluctant confession will be too late. Men have their opportunity to receive Christ today. As Paul stated in 2 Corinthians 6:2, "Behold, now is the accepted time; behold, now is the day of salvation." After death and in the consummation of human history when Christ judges the world, it will be too late. The shout of triumph of the archangel (1 Th 4:16), and the adoration of ten thousand times ten thousand saints will be sadly echoed by the cry of despair of those who have neglected the day of their salvation. How important it is to heed the admonition of Psalm 2 before the hour of divine judg-ment: "Serve the LORD with fear, and rejoice with trembling. Kiss the Son, lest he be angry, and ye perish from the way, when his wrath is kindled but a little. Blessed are all they that put their trust in him" (Ps 2:11-12).

Although not fully expressed, the apostle Paul is here exhorting the Philippians to examine their meager vessels of devotion, their limited yieldedness to the will of God, and, in response to the example of their great Saviour, to give them-selves without reserve to Him. In the light of this truth, how small were their petty differences and their selfish interests. To be Christlike means to follow His example. This be-comes the burden of the exhortation which follows.

EXHORTATION TO WORK OUT THEIR OWN SALVATION, 2:12-13

Having set forth in the previous verses the humility of Christ as their example and the exaltation of Christ as their encouragement, the apostle now proceeds to exhort them to fulfill in their lives the spiritual accomplishments which are in keeping with their faith in such a Saviour. The word *wherefore* gathers up all the preceding revelation. In ad-dressing them as "my beloved," he is appealing to their af-fection for him and his affection for them as the ground of their obedience to his exhortation rather than exercising his apostolic authority. He reminds them of their obedience in the past, with the word *always* coming prominently in the sentence. He implies that if he were present, their love for him would bring automatic obedience. But now he appeals to obedience even in his absence, with emphasis on "much more in my absence," as if under the present circumstances it is all the more important that they give heed to his exhor-tation.

The burden of his desire for the Philippian church is summarized in the exhortation, "Work out your own salvation with fear and trembling." The verb translated "work out" means "achieve" or "accomplish."[19] Although the verb comes last in the sentence, it introduces an idea which is sometimes misunderstood. Although salvation is a work of God for man in the nature of a gift, the outworking of the new life in Christ requires a response of obedience and faith on the part of the believer. While the work of Christ on the cross is the basis for all of God's redemption, the application of redemption to the individual and the achievement of spiritual victory over sin are contemporary experiences of the child of God. It is not that God gives salvation to a believer as an initial act and then requires the individual to complete the salvation. Salvation is not a stepladder which reaches from earth to heaven which is climbed by self-effort. It is rather that the salvation, which by its nature is complete and is God's provision for us, needs to be applied to the daily experience of the believer in Christ. Muller says,

> The believer is called to self-activity, to the active pursuit of the will of God, to the promotion of the spiritual life in himself, to realisation of the virtues of the Christian life, and to a personal application of salvation. He must "work out" what God in His grace has "worked in."[20]

The salvation that is here the subject of exhortation is not salvation from the guilt of sin. It is obvious that a believer in Christ is justified completely by faith, instantly and once for all, when he receives Christ as his Saviour. His new-found position in Christ can never be improved and never advances. The fact that he is in Christ, however, introduces a whole new life which by its nature is a process of experience and development. Sanctification is not only positional but experiential, and should be realized in the daily life of the believer. Only as he experiences deliverance from the power of sin and appropriates the new life in Christ does the believer actually achieve God's ultimate purpose for his present life. This is intended in the exhortation to work out our own salvation.

Obviously a person cannot work out salvation which he does not possess. We must begin with what God has so wonderfully wrought in making us children of God, assuring us of His love and care and mercy, and giving to us the indwelling presence of the Holy Spirit. Paul does not introduce this exhortation as a threat, with the penalty of disobedience being the loss of salvation. Rather, he reminds the Christians of their infinite resources in Christ and exhorts them to enjoy the riches of grace which are already theirs by right of faith in Christ.

The standard which he is urging upon them is not something new, for he says they have obeyed in the past and have already gone a long way in experiencing God's salvation. Now, however, he wants them to go still further and to perfect that which is still lacking.

In the exhortation, the expression "with fear and trembling" in the order of the Greek comes first and the verb comes last. No foes of spiritual life are more obvious than self-complacency and pride. Spiritual growth comes when we realize our need for it. No doubt the small problems that existed in the Philippian church were fostered by spiritual pride and self-congratulation. The remedy was to recognize their need and the great danger of falling short of full realization of spiritual power and victory. Fear and trembling are proper reactions as we realize our own weakness and inadequacy. The remedy is to realize the divine sufficiency of God's power.

Paul quickly points out, however, that this program of working out our own salvation is not one of self-effort, for he says, "It is God which worketh in you both to will and to do of his good pleasure" (v. 13). It is not the idea of work—that unless you work God cannot help you—but rather, work with the realization that you work not alone, that you have an infinite power within you, that actually God is working out His will for you and motivating you both to will or desire it and also to accomplish His good pleasure.

The Greek word translated "worketh in you" is the source of the English word *energy*. It is the energy or power of God which alone can both influence the will of the Christian and replace his weakness with power. The Christian life, like salvation as a whole, can only be accomplished by God's infinite power.

F. B. Meyer points out that this great text has six dominant notes: God's Personality—'it is God'; God's Immanence—'in you'; God's Energy—'worketh in you'; God's Morality—He works in you 'to will'; God's Efficiency—He works in you 'to work'; God's Ultimate Satisfaction—'for His own good pleasure.' "[21]

GREAT ESSENTIALS OF THE WILL OF GOD, 2:14-16

The several exhortations to triumphant service for God, which enlarge upon what Paul had in mind in the outworking of the believers' salvation, may at first glance seem to be relatively minor qualities. A closer examination will reveal, however, that they are symptomatic of a supernatural life in Christ achieved only by the power of God. Further, they are the particular qualities in which apparently the Philippian church had been somewhat lacking.

The first exhortation, "Do all things without murmurings and disputings," although very simple and direct, constitutes a sweeping command rarely obeyed by most Christians. As Hendriksen states, the issue is not simply obedience outwardly, but obedience inwardly, obedience which is not grudging or merely external.[22] One of the most common failures of Christians who have lost sight of the wonder of God's grace is the tendency to complain, often about simple things such as food and drink, as illustrated in the children of Israel in the wilderness. Such complaining, however, is a symptom of a deep-seated spiritual problem—failure to really trust God and failure to be submissive to His providential provision. In the case of Israel it brought forth the most severe judgment. In the lives of Christians, complaining is a symptom of being out of touch with the power of God.

The order of the words in the original in verse 14 is most significant. The word *all* stands first. Most Christians do *some* things without murmuring or arguments. The problem is to do *all* things in this spirit.

The verb *do* stands second in the sentence and significantly is in the present tense, which emphasizes that not only should they do all things without murmuring, but they should be without murmuring or disputing at all times and in all circumstances. The standard is one of complete submission to the will of God, complete confidence in His goodness, and full realization of His tremendous blessings, which would make murmuring an expression of thanklessness. What should be completely lacking in the Christian life is defined as "murmurings," significantly in the plural, and referring to all complaints and grumbling, whether expressed or unexpressed.

The word translated "disputings" is a Greek word from which the English *dialogue* comes, with the idea of reasoning, expression of opinion, and hence disputes or arguments. Although the Christian life is not unreasonable, the will of

God may seem unreasonable at times to a Christian. Whether one disputes with God or disputes with his fellow Christians, such dialogue often reflects a lack of submission to the will and revelation of God. A Christian is called to unquestioning obedience, and in his relationship to fellow Christians should not be argumentative.

The purpose of this is that there might be a complete absence of things which would mar our testimony (v. 15). A Christian, therefore, should be blameless. The verb "be" means being in the sense of becoming or achieving, and the aorist subjunctive indicates that he should be blameless in each act and each instance. It is a situation that does not arise simply from being in the sense of existence, but being in the sense of achievement.

The word *harmless* means literally, "unmixed," therefore, "pure" and "innocent of evil," whereas murmuring and disputing would bring a foreign element into what would otherwise be a pure devotion to Christ. These good qualities are becoming to those who are "children," literally, "those who are born as genuine children of God." Paul is saying that these qualities of life are outgrowths of our divine nature received in our new birth. By contrast, Israelites are declared to be no children of God in Deuteronomy 32:5 in the Septuagint rendering and, according to Christ, are a "faithless and perverse generation" (Lk 9:41).

The result will be that the believers are "without rebuke," that is, "without a blemish." Their purity of life and character would make them stand out as lights in the darkness in a world which is crooked and perverse. The word for "lights" is the same word for stars in the heavens, and could be translated "luminaries." The only other instance of this word in the Bible is found in Revelation 21:11, referring to the light of the New Jerusalem. The word *shine* is better translated "appear," although shining is implied. The world, by contrast, is "crooked," that is, "dishonest" and "perverse," an even stronger word meaning, "depraved" or "morally perverted." The world is called a "nation" in the sense of it being the present generation. The contrast between a Christian, who is completely blameless, and the world, completely perverted, is a study in opposites. While most Christians are far from being depraved in their life, any impurity for this reason stands out all the more. F. C. Synge aptly captions Philippians 2:14-18, "AVOID THE FAULTS OF ISRAEL."[23] The history of Israel is indeed a record of failure, especially in avoiding murmurings and disputings.

The qualities of life extolled in verses 14 and 15 are a platform on which Christian testimony can go forth. Ultimately, Christian testimony is more than just a life; it is a spoken word, a heralding of divine revelation. Hence in verse 16 Paul speaks of "holding forth the word of life." It is a holding out of the Word of God, an offering as one would offer food or a gift. A Christian walking in fellowship with God is in a good spiritual state to assure any who will hear that the Word of God which he is offering will satisfy the hungry heart. The expression *word of life* stands first in the sentence for emphasis. Paul anticipates that as the Philippians are faithful in preaching the Word, it may bring rejoicing to Paul himself "in the day of Christ, that I have not run in vain, neither laboured in vain." Paul not only wanted to be a benefit to the Philippians, but wanted to reach countless others through them. The gospel is only truly comprehended when it is received as a trust and stewardship, the fulfillment of which is to pass it on to others.

The expression "the day of Christ," as earlier in 1:6, 10, refers to the time when Christ will come for His church and believers will be rewarded at the judgment seat of Christ. Although many expositors identify this phrase as the day of the Lord, the context of its usage seems to refer to the blessings upon Christians rather than judgment on the world as contemplated in the day of the Lord.[24] It is at this judgment that Christian testimony will be evaluated, and Paul longs to have his own efforts not rated as "in vain" or empty. It also reminds the Philippians that their efforts will be evaluated and rewarded.

The Christian life is not only to illustrate the holiness of God, but also to run the race and win the prize (Gal 2:2; 1 Co 9:24; 2 Ti 4:7). The Lord is the Rewarder of those who diligently serve Him.

THE EXAMPLE OF PAUL, 2:17-18

The standard which Paul is holding before the Philippian church is one which he himself is willing to apply to his own life. If anyone had a right to complain, it was Paul, who had already spent years in prison as a direct result of his faithfulness to the Lord. Here, however, he states his own point of view: he is willing to die if necessary to accomplish his mission. He writes, "Yea, and if I be offered upon the sacrifice and service of your faith, I joy, and rejoice with you all." Paul had already suffered much for Christ, as outlined in 2 Corinthians 11:23-29. Now he is willing to be a sacrifice poured out, whether as a libation complementing their faith, like the drink offering of Jewish sacrifices, or in the sense of pouring out his blood. If his own suffering and even death would further the cause of the Philippian church, he is willing to submit to the will of God with joy and rejoicing. The word *service* has in view a sacred ritual or form of worship. There was more to the sacrificial system than just the sacrifice itself.

The last clause of verse 17, "with you all," suggests that Paul regards the church as a unit and is not siding with any factions. If he was serving them, he was serving them all. If he was to have joy and rejoicing in them, he would recognize God's grace in all of them.

THE EXAMPLE OF TIMOTHY, 2:19-24

Paul's concern for the Philippian church is manifested not only in this epistle and in his desire to visit them personally, but he announces that in order to learn firsthand how they are getting along he is sending Timothy to them as his personal representative. It goes without saying that Timothy would also report how the Philippians had responded to Paul's exhortations to unity. However, the coming of Timothy would be delayed until Paul learned the outcome of his trial (v. 23), so that the Philippians could also have their fears relieved.

Timothy had had a long and intimate contact with this church (Ac 16:3; 17:14-15; 19:22; 20:3-4; Phil 2:19-23), and, second to Paul, was beloved by the Philippian Christians. Accordingly, he would be most acceptable as Paul's representative.

The occasion of sending Timothy gives Paul opportunity to point to Timothy as an example of Christian faith and testimony. Although Timothy had not shared Paul's imprisonment in Rome or earlier in Philippi (Ac 16), nevertheless, by his constant waiting on Paul, he had been most faithful to the Lord. It is another reminder that God works in different lives in different ways. Although Timothy had not suffered as Paul had suffered, his testimony was nevertheless unblemished.

In commending Timothy, Paul brings out some of his sterling qualities. First he declares, "I have no man like-

minded." The word translated "likeminded" is found only
here in the New Testament and literally is "like-souled."
This should be understood, not as being simply in close bond
with Paul himself, which of course was true, but Paul is saying that none of his other followers had quite the same qualities of soul that are found in Timothy. Of all Paul's converts,
Timothy seemed to have manifested the greatest faithfulness
to the Lord as well as fidelity to Paul.

Accordingly, Paul, in sending Timothy to the Philippian
church, is able to assure them that Timothy "will naturally
care for your state." The word translated "naturally" is
the word for birthright. What Paul is implying is that in his
spiritual birth Timothy acquired a new nature which in-
stinctively would have a care for the Philippian church.
While this no doubt stems from the fact that God is Timothy's spiritual father, there is a sense also in which Paul,
through his influence on Timothy, may have instilled this
love for the saints. In any event, it is from the new nature
rather than the old.

By contrast, Paul had seen in too many of his converts
their continued selfishness, summarized in verse 21: "For
all seek their own, not the things which are Jesus Christ's."
No doubt there were individual exceptions, such as Luke,
who had also been most faithful in Rome and elsewhere; but
Paul is making a generalization. How sadly true that in the
church of Jesus Christ so few have a genuine devotion for
Christ and unselfishly serve the church.

The apostle appeals to their knowledge of Timothy serving as Paul's assistant in a close bond described as "a son
with the father" (v. 22). He did not need to say more, as
they already knew how faithful Timothy had been. In sending him to the Philippian church, Paul was in effect sending
his own son, a trusted representative who had demonstrated

not only his care for the Philippian church, but his own love and faithfulness to Paul. Paul was complimenting them by sending his most trusted assistant. Timothy's departure would be delayed only by the necessity of waiting until he could bring tidings of Paul's acquittal. Paul himself promises to come to them as soon as possible. From available evidence, however, Paul's trial was delayed longer than he anticipated at this time.

THE EXAMPLE OF EPAPHRODITUS, 2:25-30

Having set before the Philippian church not only the example of Christ, but his own life as an apostle, and Timothy's life of testimony, Paul now commends Epaphroditus, who had been sent by the Philippians to minister to him and to bring an offering. He is now being sent back to them with Paul's commendation.

Although Timothy's visit was delayed, Epaphroditus was to go immediately and bear the epistle Paul was writing. Epaphroditus, mentioned only in this chapter, bore a name commonly used and frequently found in ancient literature, sometimes in its shortened form, Epaphras.[25] He was probably a different person than the Epaphras mentioned in Colossians 1:7; 4:12; Philemon 1:23, an individual who lived in Colosse.

Epaphroditus is warmly described as a "brother, and companion in labour, and fellowsoldier, but your messenger, and he that ministered to my wants." For the apostle to recognize an ordinary layman in such high commendation was generous of Paul and also expresses his appreciation for all Epaphroditus had done.

Epaphroditus had not only brought the message and gift from the Philippian church, but he had stayed to minister to Paul. Lightfoot observes that the three words, *brother, companion,* and *fellowsoldier,* "are arranged in an ascending scale; common sympathy, common work, common danger in toil and suffering."[26] While ministering to Paul, Epaphroditus had become ill, and now both he and Paul were concerned that the Philippians would have heard reports of his illness without reports of his recovery. Paul says, "For he longed after you all, and was full of heaviness, because that ye had heard that he had been sick" (v. 26).

Paul explains that Epaphroditus had indeed been sick, in fact, had almost died, and that his recovery was an evidence of the mercy of God on him, and also on himself, lest the death of Epaphroditus would bring additional sorrow upon him in his imprisonment. Hendriksen gives a long list of beautiful passages setting forth the doctrine of the mercy of God, commenting, "God *pitied* both Epaphroditus and Paul! It is comforting to know that the heart of God is filled with *mercy,* that is, with *loving kindness* and *active pity.* In Christ he is 'touched with the feeling of our infirmities.' "[27]

The emotional bonds binding Paul and Epaphroditus to the Philippian church are evident in the verbs used. The word for "longed" (v. 26) is an intensified word indicating intense longing, and is further emphasized by the expression "full of heaviness," a strong word for distress whether physical or mental, such as extreme grief or shame. Paul's own concern at the thought of the possibility of Epaphroditus dying expressed in the term "sorrow upon sorrow" is literally "pain upon pain," such as the pain of childbirth.

Because of Paul's concern for Epaphroditus, the possible anxiety of the Philippian church regarding him, and his desire to express through Epaphroditus his love for them, he was prompted to send Epaphroditus at this time. Accordingly, Paul writes, "I sent him therefore the more carefully, that, when ye see him again, ye may rejoice, and that I may be the less sorrowful" (v. 28). The expression "the more care-fully" could have been translated "the more earnestly" or "the more diligently." The decision to send Epaphroditus was not, therefore, carelessly contrived, but grew out of the deep concern of both men for that church.

On the basis of the circumstances and the triumphant service which Epaphroditus had rendered, Paul exhorts them to "receive him therefore in the Lord with all gladness; and hold such in reputation." Apparently Epaphroditus was not among the gifted church leaders but probably would not have been classified as one of the ordinary members either. Although not a prophet or a gifted teacher, his service had been so exceptional that Paul desires it to be recognized. The church, therefore, was to extend to Epaphroditus a glad welcome and honor him as a faithful servant of Jesus Christ.

The triumphant service of Epaphroditus is summed up in verse 30: "Because for the work of Christ he was nigh unto death." Whether the extent of his service and devotion overextended him and resulted in his illness, or whether it was simply incident to his trip to Rome, is not clear. The implication is that if he had not come to Rome, he would not have become sick. However, the next phrase implies that having become ill, he continued in his service to Paul to the point of endangering his life. The phrase "not regard-ing his life" could be translated "having gambled with his life." Probably the severity of his illness, if not the illness itself, was caused by his faithfulness in serving Paul. In doing this he not only expressed his own devotion but over-exerted himself, as Paul said, "to supply your lack of service toward me." Paul was not implying that the Philippians had failed, but rather, because they were not present, Epa-phroditus as their representative stepped in the gap and did what they would have done. Epaphroditus' overexertion which complicated his illness was, in effect, his expression of the love of the Philippian church for Paul.

Chapter 2 is a telling argument in Paul's exhortation to the Philippians in their triumphant service for God to achieve the utmost in Christian love and fellowship. Not only did he hold before them the example of Christ as the ultimate pattern, but by citing three outstanding examples—his own life and testimony, and that of Timothy and Epaphroditus—he emphasized the possibility of Christians, even though frail and human, achieving a high level of Christian fellowship and mutual understanding.

The Philippian church could not hide behind a supposed impossibility in view of the human illustrations of those who had in large measure achieved "the mind of Christ." Although the apostle goes on to view other problems natural to Christian life and testimony in chapter 3, it is clear from the emphasis in the first two chapters that his primary concern was that the Philippians would walk close to the Lord and in complete loving fellowship with each other. With this experience of the grace of God, other problems could be handled as they arose.

3

TRIUMPH IN CHRIST

WARNING AGAINST JUDAISTIC TEACHERS, 3:1-3

IN BEGINNING CHAPTER 3, the apostle seems to be concluding his epistle. The first word is "finally," literally, "for the rest" or "in conclusion." This is normally the way he concludes his epistles (cf. 1 Th 4:1; 2 Th 3:1; 2 Co 13:11; Eph 6:10). However, sometimes when he appears to be concluding his epistle, he only introduces a long section, as in 1 Thessalonians. But here, Paul is obviously diverted from his intention to conclude the epistle by the pressing burden of reminding the Philippians of dangers that lurk in the way of their triumph in Christ. Robert Mounce titles this section "An Interrupted Conclusion."[1]

After the exhortation, "rejoice in the Lord," literally, "keep on rejoicing in the Lord," Paul immediately refers to what appears to be instruction previously given to them. "To write the same things to you, to me indeed is not grievous, but for you it is safe." What does he mean by "the same things"? One suggestion is that he is merely repeating what he has said earlier in the epistle, namely, to keep on rejoicing and to maintain close Christian fellowship.

But the material which follows is so different from previous exhortations that some believe Paul is referring to earlier epistles. Lightfoot, in an extended consideration of whether there were epistles written to the Philippians which are now lost, concludes there is insufficient evidence in favor of it.[2]

However, ten years had passed since Paul had first come to Philippi, and it would only be natural for letters to go back and forth to maintain the ties of friendship. Paul refers to such other epistles and his signature on them in 2 Thessalonians 3:17, and there is possible implication that there were additional letters besides 1 and 2 Thessalonians written to the Thessalonian church (2 Th 2:2, 15). In 2 Corinthians 10:10-11 there is also reference to other letters which are not now contained in the Bible.

After considering all the alternatives, however, Lightfoot finally concludes there probably is no clear evidence in this epistle itself to another letter. Contrary evidence notwithstanding, it seems difficult to believe that there would be no evidence of these letters or quotations from them in extant literature if they actually existed. While there exists a possibility and even a probability that such letters were written, the evidence is insufficient.[3]

In regard to repeating the instructions and exhortations of chapter 3, the apostle states that it is not "grievous" or "troublesome," a translation of a word meaning "lazy" or "indolent." No great effort on his part is required to repeat this instruction, and it is "safe" to do so lest they forget the dangers he is mentioning. There follows an exhortation apparently addressed against Judaizing teachers, that is, Christians attempting to put the church under Mosaic law and regulations as well as the traditions of the Jews. With this party Paul had many unpleasant dealings in Rome, as he indicated earlier in 1:15-16.

Dangers prompting the entire discussion of chapter 3 may at first glance seem quite remote to the twentieth century. The principles involved, however, are recurring problems in the church. In light of Paul's earlier rejoicing even in those who "preach Christ of contention" (1:16), it may seem that his contention in chapter 3 is unnecessarily sharp. But it is apparent that there were various degrees of problem here. If the difficulty were only disagreement with Paul, which did not hinder their preaching Christ, Paul could to some extent condone their error. When this went to the length of the error described here, it became a more serious practical and theological problem.

Translated into modern terminology and separated somewhat from its Jewish context, the error which Paul is attacking is, first of all, the obscuring of the gospel of salvation by grace alone and substituting a works principle as a basis for standing before God. Second, it was the error of using the Mosaic law as a criterion for sanctification in the age of grace. The attempt to make the Mosaic law a precise rule of conduct for Christians today continues to plague a portion of the church. The larger error of obscuring the doctrine of grace characterizes most cults and is the basic doctrine of religions other than Christianity.

As the latter part of chapter 3 makes plain, this leads to a false sense of moral attainment which obscures the true principle of triumph through the resurrection power of Christ. In its worst form it is an error which characterizes the unsaved who have religion without salvation by grace. All of this, which was dealt with earlier in the epistle to the Galatians, is now given a particular application to the problems facing the church at Philippi and the Judaizers that were located there. Accordingly, in the study of this chapter it is necessary to translate the exhortation and its first century context into the problem as it still exists today. The goal is to achieve real triumph in Christ instead of a spurious, legalistic morality.

Paul begins with the exhortation, "Beware of dogs." The word *beware* comes from the verb meaning "to see" and

Beware

hence "to look out for," "notice" or "watch for." The tense
of the verb is present, hence it means "keep on looking out
for" (cf. Mk 4:24; 8:15; Lk 21:8; 2 Jn 8). He describes
them as "dogs," a designation often used by Jews in reference to Gentiles, but referring to anyone guilty of either
moral failure or ceremonial deviation, with the basic idea of
being impure. Dogs in the ancient world were scavengers
feeding on garbage and filth, fighting among themselves and
attacking those who might pass by. The thought is that these
Judaizing teachers, like dogs, are eating the garbage from
the table instead of sitting down at the banquet table of the
grace of God. He uses the same verb for the second and
third exhortation, "Beware of evil workers," that is, those
who are guilty of evil deeds, and also to "Beware of the concision," literally, "mutilations," such as are true of heathen
religions where they cut themselves in their frenzy. William
Hendriksen points out that the threefold reiteration, "beware . . . beware . . . beware," has similar parallels in the
Scripture where other terms are repeated three times, such as
"holy" (Is 6:3), "the temple of Jehovah" (Jer 7:4), and
"land" (Jer 22:29).[4]

The "concision" is an apparent allusion to the exaltation
of circumcision, which was commanded of Jews in the Old
Testament. In the light of grace in Christ, circumcision as
a religious rite becomes only a mutilation without spiritual
benefit. The thought of mutilation is in contrast to circumcision (v. 3), which is spiritual in nature. Paul says, "For
we are the circumcision, which worship God in the spirit,
and rejoice in Christ Jesus, and have no confidence in the
flesh." Instead of relying on a rite, they were experiencing
what the rite really signified—separation to God, worship,
and rejoicing and trusting in Christ rather than having confidence in a ritual. Far more important is the spirit than the

letter, especially when the letter is misapplied in attempting to make the Mosaic law intended for the Jews under the old dispensation applicable to Christians, especially Gentiles, in the dispensation of grace.

The problem of the Judaizers was partly theological and partly practical. They had reduced Christian life to a set of rules and had neglected the heart of the matter. The danger of thus exalting what Paul calls "the flesh," the natural abilities of man, now becomes the subject of extended comment and testimony.

Muller observes three characteristics mentioned by Paul relating to those who are spiritually circumcised: (1) They "worship God in the spirit," that is, they are empowered in their spiritual life by the Holy Spirit; (2) they "rejoice in Christ Jesus" instead of glorying in their own works; (3) they "have no confidence in the flesh," that is, they fully understand that the old nature is carnal whether it refers to the physical, the intellectual, or the ceremonial.[5]

WARNING AGAINST CONFIDENCE IN THE FLESH,
3:4-6

Having warned the Philippians against legalism, Paul gives his own testimony of his deliverance from confidence in the flesh. Being a thorough student of Judaism, fully aware of all the teachings of the law, and having been zealous in its proclamation and application before he met Christ on the road to Damascus, he was in a good position to speak emphatically on this subject. "Though I might also have confidence in the flesh. If any other man thinketh that he hath where of he might trust in the flesh, I more" (v. 4). In effect, Paul now assumes the role of a Judaizer, stating that if the principle of exalting the flesh is assumed, he is in a good position to do so. Elsewhere he uses the same device, assuming

the role of his contradictors in bringing home the illogic of
their teaching (Ro 9:3-5; 11:1; 2 Co 11:21-23). In stating
causes for false confidence, a fivefold ground for trusting in
the flesh is presented and refuted:

1. *Confidence in a rite.* All Jews observed the rite of circumcision and, as a faithful Jew, Paul had fulfilled this
command given to Abraham. If anyone had a right to claim
the benefits of circumcision, Paul did. By claiming circumcision on the eighth day (actually on the seventh day as
parts of days were counted), Paul is emphasizing that he
was not a late convert to Judaism but was born and raised
in it. Converts would be circumcised as adults. In this he
may have exceeded the claims of his Judaizing opponents
who may have embraced Judaism in their mature years.[6]

2. *Confidence in race.* The Jews were naturally proud of
their descent from Abraham, Isaac, and Jacob, and looked
disparagingly on any who could not claim this lineage. Some
felt this gave them an automatic standing before God in salvation. If any should claim this, Paul said he also could
justify confidence in the flesh as he was "of the stock of
Israel, of the tribe of Benjamin, a Hebrew of the Hebrews."
Going beyond the usual claim of race, he points out that he
is from one of the best tribes—the tribe of Benjamin, which
with Judah had stood somewhat faithful to God after the
division of the kingdom. Paul was justly proud of his lineage. Beyond racial connection, however, he was a "Hebrew
of the Hebrews." This had reference to language and customs of the Jewish faith. In order to be considered a Hebrew, one had to know the Hebrew tongue and observe Hebrew customs. It, therefore, goes beyond the ordinary designation of being an Israelite (cf. 2 Co 11:22). Paul was
not only nominally a Hebrew, but was an outstanding one,
knowing the language well and speaking it fluently (Ac 21:

40; 22:2), and having studied under a great Hebrew teacher, Gamaliel (Ac 22:3), he probably was more of a Hebrew than the criticizing Judaizers. If the principles supporting Judaizing were admitted, Paul was far ahead of his critics.

3. *Confidence in religion.* When it came to observing the Mosaic law as a principle of action for the Christian, Paul points out that he was not only a learned scholar in the law, but belonged to the strictest sect, that of the Pharisees, who were fully familiar not only with the law itself but with all the traditions of the Jews that related to it. In speaking of "the law," the article is omitted in the original, which seems to indicate that he refers to the Mosaic law as a moral principle of conduct rather than as a written document. If observance of law is essential to confidence in the flesh, Paul is far superior to the Judaizers.

4. *Confidence in record.* Paul's attainments, however good on paper, were supported by active zeal in pursuing them. There is deep irony in his boasting briefly expressed here, "Concerning zeal, persecuting the church." The implication is that the Judaizers who were persecuting him were weaklings in comparison to what Paul had done when he persecuted the church. In other epistles the apostle refers to his zeal (1 Co 15:9; Gal 1:13-14). In this he far exceeded the Judaizing teachers, and his record was better than theirs.

5. *Confidence in personal righteousness.* Not only had the apostle applied the law rigorously to others, but he himself had observed its fine points. He probably was more faithful in this than the Jews who were criticizing him, even though this left him dissatisfied, which led him in Romans 7 to the conclusion, "O wretched man that I am!" (Ro 7:24). The law properly applied and interpreted could only bring condemnation, not release from guilt; but if there were right-

eousness by the law, Paul had it. Here Paul not only takes into consideration observance of "the law," but even the law principle. "Law" (without the article), even in its general application to the Christian, could only bring bondage. What Paul is making clear is that the Judaizers were not facing their own problems. The principles which they advocated did not lead either to salvation or to sanctification, as Paul discusses in Galatians. With confidence in the flesh put in its proper light, the way is now open to present the superiority of righteousness by faith in Christ.

SUPERIORITY OF RIGHTEOUSNESS BY FAITH, 3:7-9

With his right to claim superiority on the basis of circumcision, race, religion, faithful record, and personal righteousness from keeping the law, Paul now sweeps away in one broad statement all these props to human pride which supported legalism.

All his claims to human attainment had been destroyed on that road to Damascus thirty years before, and his real righteousness was accomplished simply by meeting the glorified Christ. The implication, of course, is that those who still exalt legalism have a faulty experience of Christ Himself. Their failure is not knowing the person and the work of Christ, and with it having blindness relative to the grace of God as well as their own need. As Hendriksen says,

> On the way to Damascus Paul had learned to know Jesus. Although there had been ample preparation for this knowledge—such as, Paul's acquaintance with the Old Testament, the testimonies he had heard from the lips of martyrs, their behavior under fire—when it broke in upon the soul, the experience was sudden and dramatic. . . . It was an unforgettable experience, that meeting with the ex-

alted Christ, while, a moment before, the apostle had still been breathing threatening and slaughter against Christ's Church, hence against this very Christ himself! Yes, he now *saw and heard* the actual Jesus, about whom he had been told so much.[7]

Things which the apostle considered "gain," a rare word also used in 1:21, refers to anything which would be to Paul's advantage. In his reckoning, however, he considers it a "loss," from a word originally meaning "punishment," but used in the sense of "damage" or "loss." The problem was that legal righteousness sometimes gets in the way and is actually a detriment to apprehending righteousness by faith through grace. The verb meaning "to count" or "to regard" is in the perfect tense and means that he had counted these things which were gain to him loss for Christ in the past, and is still doing so. The use of Greek tenses to emphasize a truth is carried out further in verse 8 where the present tense is used for counting loss in the expression, "I count all things but loss," emphasizing the continuity of it, and the use of the aorist in the expression "do count them but dung," meaning to do it as a definite act completely once for all. The reason Paul is willing to disregard all these human attainments is summed up in the word *Christ*. When he met Christ, all these grounds for confidence were swept away.

This is brought out more emphatically in verse 8, beginning with "Yea doubtless, and I count all things but loss for the excellency of the knowledge of Christ Jesus my Lord." The combination of articles, as Lightfoot points out, substitutes the present tense in verse 8 for the perfect or past tense of verse 7, and expands the "things" of verse 7 to "all things" in verse 8.[8] All of Paul's self-attainments and moral achievements pale into insignificance when he comes into the full knowledge of what Jesus Christ is and has done for him.

The expression "the excellency" refers to that which is placed above; therefore far surpassing that with which it is compared. The "knowledge" of Christ Jesus which he mentions indicates personal acquaintance, experiential knowledge as opposed to theoretical. Because he really knows Christ Jesus as his Lord, the surpassing qualities of Christ and His salvation make any of his own claims for righteousness insignificant.

As a matter of fact, Paul in accepting Christ turned his back on Judaism and Phariseeism and, literally, "suffered the loss of all things" (v. 8), such as standing, wealth, and position in the Jewish community. He counted all this as "dung," an expression used sometimes to refer to human excrement, but also for garbage or food thrown away from the table. In either case, it refers to that which is useless and actually contaminating and harmful; hence to be discarded in favor of Christ and what He had to offer Paul. The implication is that Judaizing, carried to its logical conclusion, makes it impossible to have what is real in Christ. The expression "that I may win Christ" is literally, "that I may gain Christ," the same word for "gain" in verb form as used in verse 7. One "gain" far exceeded the other.

What Paul gained is itemized as being, first, to "be found in him," and, second, to possess "the righteousness which is of God by faith" (v. 9) rather than of the law. In speaking of being "found in him," while a present reality, Paul contemplates God's ultimate decision when God will judge him. In contrast to any righteousness, supposed or otherwise, which Paul may have had related to keeping and observing the law of Moses, Paul extols righteousness which is perfect and complete, accomplished for him by Jesus Christ in His person and work. This is reckoned to Paul's account not on the basis of his personal righteousness but "by faith." While Paul compares legal righteousness with righteousness by faith and by grace, actually what he is saying is that there is no real comparison. One is worthless in comparison to the other, which is of infinite worth.

SUPERIORITY OF THE RESURRECTION POWER OF CHRIST, 3:10-11

The fact that righteousness by faith in Christ is perfect and complete refers to Paul's position in Christ to which nothing can be added. However, there is recognition that experientially there is room for growth and development. This will come, however, not through observance of legalistic standards, but rather through knowing Christ experientially. This is expressed in Paul's goal, "That I may know him, and the power of his resurrection" (v. 10). In this he states his goal to be to know Christ completely, not simply as the Justifier, but also as the Sanctifier. While righteousness came from the sacrifice of Christ on the cross, the power of God is demonstrated in the resurrection of Christ.

The chronological order is reversed in verse 10 in that resurrection is mentioned first and Christ's sufferings and death, second and third. While Christ suffered first and then was resurrected, what Paul is referring to is the order of human experience. This begins by knowing Christ in His person and work on the cross, is followed by the experience of the power of His resurrection, and then issues in the capacity to have fellowship with the sufferings of Christ (cf. Col 1: 24; 2 Ti 2:12; 1 Pe 4:13), and ends in conformity to the will of God expressed in the death of Christ (2 Co 4:10-12). All this Paul desires to know experientially, the same word for "knowledge" used in verse 8.

The Greek language used in the New Testament was well adapted to express fine distinctions in abstract thought, and Paul had a choice of several words for knowledge. He could have used *oida,* which means "to comprehend mentally," as used in 1 Thessalonians 1:4 where he states, "Knowing, brethren beloved, your election of God." Election of God by its nature is not an experience but is accepted by faith and is an intellectual concept.

Another concept for the idea of knowledge is found in Acts 10:28, where the Greek word *epistomai,* meaning "to know by acquaintance, by familiarity, or contact" is used. In Ephesians 5:17 still another Greek word, *suniemi,* is used for knowledge as it refers to a deep insight based on a logical analysis of facts. Although all these words were available to Paul, he used the common word meaning "to know experientially." Although other forms of knowledge may be involved in the Christian faith, it is evident that here he emphasized knowing Christ in a personal way. This is especially in reference to knowing the power of the resurrection of Christ which the apostle feels is the key to an adequate fellowship of His sufferings and the end result of being made comformable unto His death.

However, as noted earlier, the order of experience is different than the order of the event. Christ suffered first, died, and then was resurrected. The order of Christian experience after being saved is to know resurrection power first, and by this means to enter into the fellowship of Christ's sufferings and to be conformed to the will of God represented in the death of Christ. Although Christians cannot participate in what Christ suffered on the cross, in the endurance of suffering such as Paul had experienced there was a fellowship or a sharing of such suffering as may be necessary in each case in the will of God. As A. R. Fausset points out, fellowship with the sufferings of Christ is both by identification and experience, "by identification with Him in His sufferings and death, *by imputation;* also, in *actually bearing* the cross laid on us, after His example, so 'filling up that which is behind of the afflictions of Christ' (Col. i.24)."[9]

The ultimate purpose of experiential knowledge of the power of Christ's resurrection (v. 10) is to make possible Paul's attaining "unto the resurrection of the dead" (v. 11). As W. E. Vine observes, "The 'if' introduces not a condition but a contingency, (more lit., 'if somehow')."[10] What did Paul mean by stating as his hope that through these means he would attain unto the resurrection of the dead? The expression "the resurrection" is a translation of an unusual word found only here in the New Testament which means a "resurrection out from among." To the usual word for resurrection is added the prefix *ek,* which is further supported by a second *ek,* meaning "out of," making the entire phrase translated literally, "the resurrection out from among, the one from the dead."

In contrast to the concept of a general resurrection, Paul is anticipating here that there will be a special resurrection of the righteous which will take them out of the total number of those dead in a special act of God. This is, of course, supported in Revelation 20 by the fact that the wicked dead are not raised until the end of the thousand-year reign of Christ, whereas the righteous dead are resurrected before it. C. J. Ellicott states,

> As the context suggests, the *first* resurrection (Rev. xx.5), when, at the Lord's coming, the dead in Him shall rise first (I Thessalon. iv.16), and the quick be caught up to meet Him in the clouds (I Thess. iv.17); compare Luke xx.35. The first resurrection will include only true believers, and

will apparently precede the second, that of non-believers and disbelievers, in point of time.[11]

More specifically, Paul has in view the rapture, the event described in 1 Thessalonians 4:13-18, which is a special resurrection for those "in Christ."

If the rapture is Paul's goal here, and is that referred to as "the resurrection of the dead," why did he feel that he had to struggle to attain unto it? The best explanation seems to be that at this point he still hoped to be living at the time of the rapture of the church, and therefore his hope that he "might attain" unto the event means in effect that he would still be alive rather than resurrected with those who had died. Ellicott's observation that Paul's uncertainty was "an expression, not so much of doubt, as of humility," is not the point he is making.[12] As Fausset states, it is "not implying uncertainty of the issue, but the earnestness of the struggle (1 Cor. ix.26, 27), the need of jealous self-watchfulness (1 Cor. x.12), and the indefatigable use of means at all cost."[13] In view of Paul's total doctrine of grace and his assurance of salvation stated so emphatically in a passage like 2 Timothy 1:12, it is hardly plausible that Paul had any uncertainty about his ultimate resurrection if he died. The only question was whether he would still be living when the rapture occurred. Later it was revealed to him that he would die a martyr's death.

Accordingly, Paul endured his suffering in prison with the thought from day to day that possibly this would be cut short by the Lord's return and his immediate deliverance. His endurance of sufferings, therefore, would become a means to the end that he might live until that glad day. Christians today who endure sufferings and who are undergoing great trial can have the same hope of deliverance and, like Paul, are entitled to look for the blessed hope of Christ's return.

THE TRUE MEANING OF PERFECTION, 3:12-16

One of the natural longings arising from the spiritual experience of conversion is the desire to perfect one's spiritual life. In this outgrowth of having become a new creature in Christ with a new nature longing after the things of God, it is easily possible to go to extremes. On the one hand, discontent with one's spiritual life can bring discouragement and unnecessary resignation to spiritual defeat. On the other hand, in overestimating one's spiritual attainments, it is easy to become complacent with the measure of transformation which has taken place. Either alternative is falling short of the scriptural standard. What Paul is teaching in this section is that absolute perfection, such as exists in heaven, or attainment of spiritual victory which makes defeat impossible, is never achieved in this life. But there is the possibility of a high plateau of victory in Christ, of joy in the Spirit, and of the satisfaction of having served the Lord acceptably. It is this proper doctrine that the apostle is attempting to teach in this section.

Undoubtedly the introduction of this subject is prompted by the Judaizers in Rome who had adopted a legalistic approach to life which all too easily fosters pride in human attainment and disparagement of other Christians who may not have fully matured spiritually. Legalism tends to enthrone a system of conduct which the legalizer feels he has attained. Too often it contains regulations more strict than the Scriptures themselves, while ignoring other plain admonitions in the Word of God. The legalizer, basking in the supposed superiority of his own spiritual attainment, often is far less spiritually minded than the one whom he judges so severely. Paul is contending against this form of error by giving his own personal testimony of spiritual victory on the one hand, and urging continual striving for further progress on the other.

He begins by saying, "Not as though I had already attained, either were already perfect" (v. 12). The perfection he would have at the future resurrection was not yet attained, as he still had a sin nature, a sinful body, and was only too aware of the need for further spiritual progress. In stating that he was not already perfect, the apostle Paul used a Greek word *teleioo,* meaning "to reach a goal" or "fulfill a purpose." The Greek word is the root of the English word *teleology* which refers to the design or purpose of the universe. The same word is found in Luke 13:32; John 17:23; 1 Corinthians 2:6; 2 Corinthians 12:9; Ephesians 4:12, and many other passages.

Another word for spiritual perfection not occurring in Philippians is the Greek word *katartizo* which refers to completeness in all details, as in a well-furnished room. This word is used in such passages as 2 Corinthians 13:11; 1 Thessalonians 3:10; Hebrews 13:21; 1 Peter 5:10. Neither of the words, however, refers to sinless perfection, and both imply a process of attainment.

In the Scripture, perfection is revealed to be in three stages:

1. Positional perfection as it relates to our salvation has already been given to every true Christian, as stated in Hebrews 10:14, "For by one offering he hath perfected for ever them that are sanctified."

2. Progressive or relative perfection is related to maturity in the spirituality spoken of in 2 Corinthians 7:1 as "perfecting holiness in the fear of God." Various aspects of such perfection are mentioned in the Bible, such as holiness (2 Co 7:1), love (1 Jn 5:17-18), patience (Ja 1:4), the will of God in general (Col 4:12), and accomplishing "every

good work" (Heb 13:21). Although legalists sometimes imagine themselves perfect, as was true of the Galatian church, they were far from perfect. Paul, chiding the Galatian church, asked, "Are ye so foolish? Having begun in the Spirit, are ye now made perfect [literally, "Are ye now being made perfect"] by the flesh?" (Gal 3:3). The Christian life consists in growth in grace and in perfecting what is lacking, and to this end God has given to Christians various spiritual gifts "for the perfecting of the saints" (Eph 4:12).

3. Although the Bible usually refers to perfection as either positional or progressive, there are references to ultimate perfection which will be realized in heaven (Eph 5:27). Although moral perfection is ever the goal in the Christian life, the apostle Paul, like the apostle John (1 Jn 1:8-10), disclaims having achieved it. It is this ultimate moral perfection which he declares, "I follow after, if that I may apprehend that for which also I am apprehended of Christ Jesus."

The tenses of the verbs in verse 12 are significant. "Perfect" is in the perfect tense, as if to say that he was not perfected once for all when he was converted. The verb *follow* is present tense and could be translated, "But I am continuing to follow after." The word *attained* is in the aorist, speaking of a specific event in the past. Paul is saying in effect, "I did not attain perfection by a single act in the past, I was not perfected in the past and still am not perfect, but it is a continual exercise of my life to pursue perfection in the hope that I 'may apprehend,' or 'seize' or 'make my very own' that for which I have been seized by Christ." In other words, it was his desire to achieve perfection in the sense of fulfilling God's purpose in his life.

He continues, "Brethren, I count not myself to have apprehended" (v. 13). Here he uses the perfect tense mean-

ing, "I count not myself to have been perfected once for all."
Paul is clearly denying sinless perfection or having experientially achieved complete holiness. He makes this a statement addressed to "brethren," with an evident attempt to
gain their attention by direct address. Instead of claiming
complete attainment, he states that the main purpose of his
life is to press on. In order to accomplish this, he makes it
his supreme purpose: "This one thing I do." It requires his
looking to the future rather than to the past, "forgetting those
things which are behind." The word "forgetting" is in the
present tense, indicating that he "keeps on forgetting" the
things which are behind. Instead of looking back, he is
"reaching forth unto those things which are before," literally,
"keeps on reaching" for it, with the verb also in the present
tense.

In verse 14 he states, "I press toward the mark for the
prize of the high calling of God in Christ Jesus." The word
for "press" is the same word translated "follow after" in verse
12, and again is in the present tense, indicating continued action, "I keep on pressing toward the mark." Like a runner,
he is concentrating every effort to reach "the mark," that is,
the goal which means to him "the prize" such as would be
awarded in a contest. The same word is used by Paul in 1
Corinthians 9:24 when he writes, "Know ye not that they
which run in a race run all, but one receiveth the prize?"
The prize at the end of the race here is "the high calling of
God," literally, the upward call.

Paul is obviously projecting himself forward to the time
of the resurrection of the dead and the rapture of the living
church, a time when both living and dead will meet the Lord
in the air and triumphantly proceed to heaven (1 Th 4:13-
18). Until that day he will not have fully attained his goals,
being still confined to a body which he describes as "the body

of this death" (Ro 7:24), still plagued with physical suffering and the advancing limitations of age. These are all part of the race as far as Paul is concerned, but, like a runner, his prime interest is in attaining the prize and finishing the race.

Having given his own testimony, he now makes the application and exhortation. He addresses this to those whom he describes as "perfect." "Let us therefore, as many as be perfect, be thus minded." Here Paul uses the adjective in contrast to the verb which appeared in verse 12. By "perfect" reference is made to being "mature," as it is translated in the Amplified Bible. Muller interprets the perfection of verse 15 as "principal perfection, which all believers in Christ possess," in contrast to "the ethical perfection towards which all must constantly strive, and of which no one can boast that he has already attained it."[14] Vine, considering perfection in verse 15 as maturity, quotes Augustine as saying that believers may be " 'perfect travellers, but not perfect possessors.' "[15]

Taking into consideration that some Christians are obviously immature and far from the goal, other Christians have attained a relative maturity or are full-grown. This does not mean that they are sinlessly perfect or do not have further progress to achieve in their spiritual lives; but relatively speaking, they are mature in spiritual things, they are full-grown much in the sense that a person having passed through the stages of childhood reaches the maturity of manhood. To such he addresses the exhortation to follow his example, "Be thus minded," that is, to have the same mind or opinion as Paul. He promises that if they are of other opinions that God will reveal the truth to them. Paul implies that if they have other opinions, they have somehow missed the full revelation of God on this point. Although they are mature Christians, remaining imperfections need to be taken away.

In verse 16 he sums up the matter to the effect that what has already been attained should be continued, as expressed in the Berkeley Version "But we must hold on to what we have attained." The best Greek manuscripts omit the last clause, "Let us mind the same thing."

Taken as a whole, this passage is a great corrective to any who may be self-satisfied with their spiritual progress, whether due to indifference or to supposed attainment of moral standards of their own erection. On the other hand, it makes clear that absolute moral perfection is not for this world, and only by continual effort can we achieve even a relative maturity. The ultimate goal of being perfect in God's presence in heaven is the prospect which spurs on the apostle in his pursuit of spiritual maturity.

EXHORTATION TO FOLLOW PAUL, 3:17-19

Although he had dealt somewhat gently with his enemies in the preceding section, Paul now sharply rebukes those who are, as a matter of fact, "the enemies of the cross of Christ." Here he is not referring simply to Christians who are misled into legalism, but to those who actually are not Christians, who either by false religion or no religion at all are impelled to contend against the Christian faith.

He begins, "Brethren, be followers together of me" (v.17). In the Greek, emphasis is made on the verb *be followers,* literally, "keep on being imitators of me." The verb *be* in the sense of "becoming" is in the present tense and speaks of continued action. The English word *imitators* is a transliteration of the Greek word with the preposition *with* added to it, hence meaning that they be imitators together. They are to "mark" or beware of those who walk otherwise, in view of the fact that they have Paul and others like him for their example.

Who are these whom Paul is denouncing? Some have taken it as another reference to the Judaizers (Christians who were attempting to live under the Jewish law and who opposed Paul's freedom in grace). Others, like Lightfoot, believe the reference is to the antinomian party—severe reactionists against the law of Moses who resented moral restraints.[16]

Vine agrees with Lightfoot that those whom Paul is denouncing here are

> antinomian errorists who taught much the same doctrines as became prominent later among the Gnostics, as that matter is evil, and that therefore the body can never be holy. Of such the Apostle writes in Rom. 16:18. Such introduced and defended immoral teachings in Corinth. They would form a separate sect at Philippi from the Judaizers, though both would find common ground in opposing the gospel.[17]

It is clear from verses 18 and 19 that Paul is not talking simply about erring Christians, but those who actually are not Christians at all. Although the error of these false teachers is disguised in the form of religion, Paul with aching heart and with tears repeats what he had told the Philippians before, that such "are the enemies of the cross of Christ." His reference to his frequent warnings apparently goes beyond this epistle itself and may refer to his instructions to them when he had been with them previously.

Having referred to these as "enemies of the cross of Christ," the apostle pronounces a fourfold indictment: (1) he describes their end as being destruction, that is, eternal punishment; (2) their "God is their belly," a description which better suits the antinomian party than it does the legalizers, although the same description is given of people who sow dissension (Ro 16:18); (3) their glory is their shame, that is, their shameless conduct is a matter of pride to them; (4) they "mind earthly things," living for the things of this life only.

Although Muller attempts to justify this scathing denunciation as applying to the Judaizing party, it would better fit the group in Philippi who were incipient Gnostics, the opposite of legalizers, and who tended to throw off moral restraints.[18]

The recurring problem of evil men who oppose the gospel and deprecate the cross was all too common in the ancient world, even as it is today. Paul's attitude, however, is not one of self-righteous condemnation of these who have not known the grace of God. With sorrowful heart he contemplates their ultimate judgment at the hand of God in the words, "whose end is destruction." Such must necessarily be the lot of those who make their appetite their god, who glorify their shame, and who continually think on things relating to this earth.

What a tragic summary of the mind of this world as contrasted to the mind of God. The Christian walk, however imperfect and falling short, is far different from the life of the worldling who knows nothing of the grace of God and whose course is steadily downward rather than upward. Although complete perfection is not for this world, Christians can know and rejoice in a measure of spiritual progress, growth in grace, and a sense of spiritual values which sees through the empty glitter of this world into the eternal and abiding values of the will of God. There is real triumph in Christ.

LOOKING FOR THE SAVIOUR, 3:20-21

The hopeless future of the lost is contrasted to the glorious prospects which face the Christian in the concluding verses of this chapter. The hope of the Christian is based first upon the fact that heaven is his home and that his real citizenship is there. His "conversation," better translated "our commonwealth" or "our citizenship," comes from a Greek word which "denotes a colony of foreigners."[19] To put it in less technical language, a Christian is assured that, in contrast to those just denounced, his real home is in heaven and that he is only temporarily related to this world, its governments, and its problems.

It is from heaven rather than from earth that a Christian may be expecting the coming of his Lord as stated by Paul, "From whence also we look for the Saviour, the Lord Jesus Christ." According to John 14:2, Christ is in heaven preparing the place for His future bride, the church. Accordingly, in keeping with the promise of John 14:3, He is coming again for His church, and hence the church can be looking to the heavens for the return of their Saviour.

The ultimate process of perfection to which Paul had alluded earlier in this chapter will also have its consummation at the time when Christ comes for His own. At that time, Christ "shall change our vile body, that it may be fashioned like unto his glorious body, according to the working whereby he is able even to subdue all things unto himself" (3:21).

Here attention is directed to the obvious fact that our body is "vile," that is, our "humble" or "lowly" body, our "body of humiliation." Our body needs to be changed by an act of God. This puts attaining perfection beyond the power of any Christian as long as he has his present body. Paul does not dwell here upon the sinfulness of the body, its mortality, or decay, but sums it all up as a body of humiliation suited for this life but not for glory. When the Lord comes, this body will be transformed into a body like the glorious body of Christ. The Greek word translated "change" means "to fashion anew" or "transform." The result is that it will be "fashioned like unto his glorious body," literally, "to be formed after the body of His glory."

The first verb seems to refer to a complete change; the second to the outer appearance or form. This dramatic transformation will be "according to the working," or "according to the energy" or "working within" of His power. The English word *energy* comes from the word translated "the working," and the verb "he is able" is the root of the English word *dynamite*. The "working" is the manifestation and the fact that "he is able" refers to the power. The result is that "he is able even to subdue all things unto himself," that is, bring all things into subjection to His authority.

The contrast between the hope of the Christian as set forth in verses 20 and 21, and the hope of those whom he has warned against in the preceding verses is most significant. One of the marks of a Christian who is occupied with his Lord is that he is eagerly waiting His return. In contrast to the antinomian party who lived for the present world and indulged their present wicked body, a Christian is occupied with his coming Lord and his promised deliverance when he will receive a glorious body suited for the presence of the Lord. One of the besetting sins of Christians in which they too much emulate the world is preoccupation with present sensual satisfaction and too little occupation with the coming of the Lord. How dramatic is Paul's description of Christians in 2 Timothy 4:8, as those "that love his appearing." Eager expectation of the return of the Lord and of the fulfillment of promises for our glorification is the hallmark of Christians walking in fellowship with their Lord. It is then that our longing for perfection will be realized.

It is clear here, as earlier in the chapter, that attaining perfection prior to this climactic event in the life of a Christian is an impossibility. A Christian can be assured, however, that his strivings and longings for perfection in this life, although only partially realized, will some day be satisfied when he stands in God's presence. Then, as the apostle John expresses it, "we shall be like him; for we shall see him as he is" (1 Jn 3:2). As Hendriksen has well summarized Christian hope,

> The citizens of the kingdom of heaven, looking *away from* all sinful pleasures, *eagerly* yearn *to welcome* their Savior, the Lord Jesus Christ. They await His manifestation in glory (I Cor. 1:7; Col. 3:4). It is awaiting *in faith* (Gal. 5:5) with *patient endurance* (Rom. 8:25), and *unto salvation* (Heb. 9:28).[20]

Triumph in Christ is assured those who put their trust in Him.

Although chapter 3 of Philippians is largely a digression after the initial exhortation to rejoice, nevertheless it indirectly provides many causes for rejoicing. Prominent in the chapter is Paul's confidence in the present grace of God to cause triumph in Christ, in the power of God to provide for present and future needs, and in the certainty of ultimate glory in the presence of Christ. The prospects of Christian hope which brought its bright rays of comfort and assurance to Paul, chained as he was to a guard representing Roman authority and limited in his movements and activities, have through the centuries brought renewed courage to all Christians suffering for Christ's sake. In a modern world which has so many evidences of the wickedness of man and the transitory glory of man's attainments, the same principles which encouraged Paul can encourage us today to triumph in Christ. Our hope, like his, whether we are in prison or in freedom, is to be looking for our Saviour from heaven. It is only then that our hearts which long for perfection will attain the full experience of being like Him.

4

TRIUMPH IN ANXIETY

KEEPING PEACE IN THE CHURCH, 4:1-3

THE FINAL CHAPTER of the epistle to the Philippians is one of the great discourses on the doctrine of peace, such as Psalm 23 in the Old Testament and John 14 in the New Testament. As the outline indicates, Paul expresses in this chapter his primary concern that the Philippians will experience wonderful peace in their relationship to the Lord and to each other in triumphing over anxiety. One of his important objectives in the epistle is to bring the Philippian Christians closer together in a peaceful and loving relationship to each other. This was first in his list of prayer petitions in 1:9, and now is made more specific in his exhortation to Euodias and Syntyche in 4:2. This is followed by the exhortation to pray with thanksgiving to achieve peace of heart, with further instruction on how to have peace of mind in 4:8-9. The occasion of their offering which they sent by Epaphroditus to Paul prompts an extended discourse on peace of mind in relation to things and circumstances as being the will of God. Paul as a prisoner who knew the depths of suffering is well qualified to discuss the experience of peace which he desires the Philippian Christians to have. In a modern context when many Christians experience anxiety, this chapter becomes an important revelation from God for mental and emotional health in a tension-filled world.

In the opening verses of chapter 4, the digression from his

concluding remarks which began in 3:1 is brought to an end and he resumes the exhortation to rejoice in verse 4, first introduced in 3:1. In the digression he had poured out his heart in warning his beloved brethren in Philippi against Judaistic teachers and against confidence in the flesh, and had extolled the superiority of righteousness by faith, the resurrection power of Jesus Christ, and the need for experiencing spiritual maturity. Now the climax to this exhortation is presented and again Paul declares his love for the Philippians.

Gathering in all the preceding exhortation and the reminder of glory ahead in the word *therefore,* the apostle addresses them as "my brethren," and adds "dearly beloved and longed for, my joy and crown." The expression "dearly beloved" is the translation of the Greek word *agapetoi,* the most emphatic word for deep and abiding love. It is used when the Father addresses the Son in Matthew 3:17: "This is my beloved Son, in whom I am well pleased" (cf. Mt 12:18; 17:5; Mk 1:11; 9:7; 12:6; Lk 3:22; and some texts of Lk 9:35). To this verbal adjective Paul adds the expression "longed for," from an adjective which expresses strong yearning; it does not occur elsewhere in the New Testament. He not only loved them dearly, but longed to see them face to face and have fellowship with them.

To this accumulation of words expressing his love, he adds, "my joy and crown" (cf. 1 Th 2:19). Their spiritual progress and love for him had brought real joy to him; but as he anticipated the coming of the Lord mentioned in 3:20-21, he contemplated that the Philippian church would also be his crown, from the Greek word *stephanos.* This indicated a crown of victory rather than "a regal or priestly diadem," and was the kind of reward an athlete would receive for winning a race (cf. 1 Co 9:24-27).[1]

It is with this background of the deepest kind of love and yearning for them that he comes next to the exhortation for which he had been preparing his readers. First, he exhorts them to "stand fast in the Lord," and again addresses them as "my dearly beloved." Obviously it would be only as the Philippian church stood fast in the Lord that they would continue to be his joy and would ultimately become his crown at the judgment seat of Christ. Standing fast in the Lord implied that their lives would be in keeping with this relationship.

Then he directs a special word of exhortation to Euodias and Syntyche, apparently two prominent women in the church (v. 2). His exhortation is to the point that they be "of the same mind in the Lord." It is probable that the hints of church disharmony to which Paul had frequently alluded earlier in the epistle (1:9, 27; 2:1-4, 5, 14) had some relationship to these two individuals. The Scriptures do not tell us what the difficulty was; but although women did not have a place of leadership in the church, their influence was nevertheless sufficient to introduce an element of disharmony. While there does not seem to have been a real clash or serious church schism, their differences apparently did affect the close spirit of fellowship and harmony that should characterize the people of God.

Paul is careful not to take sides, and his exhortation points out that if they both have the mind of the Lord the disharmony will disappear. In every work of God human personalities can sometimes introduce elements of disharmony. A common faith in Christ and a common desire to serve Him do not necessarily adjust personal differences and do not always unite everyone in a course of action. The road to smoothing out these differences is found when Christians achieve "the same mind in the Lord." When this is realized, differences in minor details of doctrine and in practical matters can be adjusted. But too often human pride, the stubbornness of the flesh, and personal ambition for prominence get in the way. Paul's exhortation emphasizes that Christians who are really yielded to the Lord should be able to resolve their differences. Even though they may not all be of precisely the same opinion, they should be able to find a meeting place in the mind of the Lord.

The exhortation to Euodias and Syntyche is followed by an entreaty addressed to one entitled a "true yokefellow." This exhortation addressed to an individual, as is verse 2, is complicated by the lack of a specific name. Muller thinks that the word *syzygus,* translated "yokefellow," is a proper name of someone in the Philippian church.[2] Such a name, however, has not been found anywhere else in Greek literature. Other suggestions have been made that the descriptive title may refer to Timothy, Silas, Paul's wife, or the husbands of Euodias and Syntyche. The best solution is that it is addressed to Epaphroditus who would carry this letter to the Philippian church. As Lightfoot expresses it, "On the whole however it seems most probable that Epaphroditus, the bearer of the letter, is intended; for in his case alone there would be no risk of making the reference unintelligible by suppression of the name."[3]

Upon his return to Philippi, Epaphroditus was accordingly instructed to "help those women which laboured with me in the gospel, with Clement also, and with other my fellow-labourers" (v. 3). It is possible that some of the dissatisfaction in the Philippian church had been because of the failure to recognize the proper place of women, either by giving them more authority than they should have, or by failing to give them their due recognition. Although it is quite clear that Paul did not recognize women as having an equal place with men and did not authorize them to be public evangelists or to assume a place commonly held by men in the church, it is most significant that he does refer to them as those who "laboured with me in the gospel," apparently much as some of the men had been fellow laborers. While they had not usurped the place of a man, they had supplemented Paul's ministry, no doubt especially in reaching women and children, and had labored with Clement and others. Such labors were to be recognized.

In addition to recognizing the ministry of women in the church, the apostle also mentions that their "names are in the book of life." No explanation is given to the reference to the book of life, but the obvious implication is that it refers to those who are saved (cf. Ex 32:32; Dan 12:1; Lk 10:20; Rev 3:5; 13:8; 20:12). Some regard the book of life as containing the names of all people who are born from which are deleted those who are unsaved. Others prefer to regard it as a book containing the names of those who are saved only. In the end, the meaning is about the same. The point here is that the women who labored with Paul would have their names equally inscribed in the book of life with men who had preached the gospel.

In general, both the exhortation to Euodias and Syntyche and the exhortation to give due recognition to those who labored in the gospel are designed to set at rest any feeling of lack of due recognition of position or attainment and to achieve a healing of the disharmony which seems to have existed in the Philippian church. The fact that service for the Lord is duly recognized also tends to quiet any feeling that others might purposely be ignoring the situation in order to achieve more recognition for themselves, and it serves to warm the hearts of all concerned.

KEEPING PEACE IN THE HEART, 4:4-7

Disharmony in the church often is the by-product of internal, personal conflicts, and Paul now directs his exhortation to the inner state of peace. Once again he urges them to rejoice—not only a renewal of the rejoicing exhorted in 3:1, but a repetition of the note sounded in 1:18 and 2:18. The Greek word for "rejoice," as Lightfoot points out, "combines a parting benediction with an exhortation to cheerfulness. It is neither 'farewell' alone, nor 'reioice' alone "[4] Vincent calls the exhortation to rejoice "the keynote of the epistle."[5]

The form of "rejoice" is present imperative and could be translated, "Keep on rejoicing in the Lord always." This is repeated: "And again I say, Rejoice," literally, "Again I will say, keep on rejoicing." While he desires them to have the joy of the Christian life, their rejoicing will also contribute to peace and harmony in the church and will aid attainment of an inner tranquility without which outer peace is an impossibility. Those who have inner peace and are rejoicing in the Lord have a predisposition to harmony with other Christians.

Along with rejoicing he exhorts them, "Let your moderation be known unto all men. The Lord is at hand." The Greek word translated "moderation" literally means "gentleness," "forbearance," or "reasonableness." Arndt and Gingrich translate it, "clemency, gentleness, graciousness."[6] The word occurs frequently in Greek literature and twice in the New Testament (Ac 24:4, translated "clemency," and 2 Co 10:1, translated "gentleness"). In contrast to the unreasonable demands upon others sometimes voiced by those who do not have the mind of Christ, a Christian should be characterized as one who is gentle and forbearing in his attitude toward others, and who is reasonable in his demands.

The apostle wants this to be well known as a Christian attitude, not only among Christians, but "unto all men."

This exhortation is supported by the reminder that the coming of the Lord is "at hand" or "near." Our judgment of others is tempered by the fact that God will need to judge us, and consciousness of our own failures and limitations tends to make us more patient with others who may fall short. Such an attitude will not only reveal a work of grace in the heart of the individual Christian, but will provide an atmosphere for harmonious relationships within the church.

The joy in a Christian's relation to God, expressed in rejoicing and the gentle spirit in relation to fellow Christians, indicates the fruit of the Spirit. This is now the basis of Paul's exhortation to faithful prayer which is also undoubtedly an essential to peace in the church. Verse 6 contains one of the great prayer exhortations in the Bible, beginning with the sweeping affirmation, "Be careful for nothing." The verb, referring to anxious care such as harasses conscientious Christians, makes clear that this kind of anxiety is to have no place in a Christian's life. The apostle uses the present imperative to indicate that we should *never* be filled with anxious care, but rather should present our needs to the Lord. Prayer is commanded as the alternative to anxious care: "But in everything by prayer and supplication with thanksgiving let your requests be made known unto God." Paraphrased, the exhortation is that in all circumstances one should present his needs in petition to the Lord in prayer, making known his particular requests to God. The verb in the present imperative implies that we should continually be presenting these requests to the Lord.

Three different words are used for prayer. First, the ordinary word for prayer is used; then "supplication," meaning the act of asking for things; and then the word "requests," referring to particular petitions. This should be accompanied "with thanksgiving," both for the fact that we can pray and present our petitions to the Lord, and for the assurance that God will hear and answer prayer. Vincent quotes Rilliet, "that the Christian, 'being, as it were, suspended between blessings received and blessings hoped for, should always give thanks and always ask.'"[7] Prayer is by faith, thanking God in advance that He will hear and answer our prayers.

The result will be not only that God will respond to our prayers, but the immediate result will be that the intercessor will receive "the peace of God." This is something more than having peace with God, referring to the position of a Christian in Christ, which is true of all true Christians. Here the reference is to the experience of this peace, a peace which is characteristic of God Himself, referred to by Christ in the words, "Peace I leave with you, my peace I give unto you" (Jn 14:27). But the peace is also *from* God, a fruit of the Spirit and a work of God in the heart.

The peace of God which comes as a result of prayer is further described by Paul as that "which passeth all understanding," and that which "shall keep your hearts and minds through Christ Jesus." Muller comments that this peace of God

> probably means that the peace which God gives excels and surpasses all our own intellectual calculations and considerations, all our contemplations and premeditated ideas of how to get rid of our cares—and which after all *cannot* completely remove our faint-heartedness and worry, and restore peace and calm to our minds. What God gives, surpasses all that we ask or think (cf. Eph. 3:20).[8]

This surpassing peace, then, is beyond human comprehension or anything that the mind could conceive of by it-

self. It is superhuman rather than purely psychological, and
is unexplainable by natural forces. As such it will "guard"
or "stand guard" against anxieties which would normally
attack the heart and mind of a Christian. By reference to
the heart, the thought is expressed that the essential nature
of man, which is both emotional and intellectual, will be
protected; and that particularly the mind, the thinking faculty which normally would reasonably consider the problems
of life, would also be garrisoned by peace. Although psychology and rational approaches to life may solve some
problems and enable us to see things in their proper light,
their capacity is mostly by way of analysis and human solution. What Paul is proposing is a supernatural peace, a
fruit of the Spirit (Gal 5:22), a peace which exists where
the circumstances cannot be changed and, where left to normal solutions, a Christian would be left in despair and
anxiety. Without question many Christians have not ade-
quately availed themselves of this provision of God for the
peace of heaven in the heart which can be obtained long
before the Christian is taken to heaven. Those who are at
peace with themselves have a proper platform on which to
build a relationship of peace and harmony with others. Too
often inner friction results in outer friction. Keeping peace
in the heart will help keep peace in the church.

KEEPING PEACE OF MIND, 4:8-9

The peace of God realized through prayer and faith has
many by-products, and one of these is that it transforms the
thought life of the child of God, giving peace of mind. That
which is in keeping with the peace of God is now the subject
of exhortation in verse 8. Again the apostle introduces the
word "finally," as in 3:1, indicating his desire to close the
epistle. Accordingly, verse 8 is a summary of the qualities

which should characterize a Christian in his thought life: meditation on the true, the honest, the just, the pure, the lovely, things of good report, and virtue and praise. His exhortation is, literally, "Keep on thinking about these things." By "thinking" he means to "consider, ponder, let one's mind dwell on."[9]

The formula implies that the best way to keep out sinful thoughts and things which disturb inner peace is to concentrate on good things, beginning with the truth; then thoughts that are honest or honorable, things that are just or right, things that are pure or holy, things that are lovely or pleasing, things of good report or good repute; if there be any moral excellence, anything worthy of praise, these are the things which should occupy our mind. So many spiritual problems and difficulties in mental health would be solved for Christians if they would follow Paul's simple exhortations in verses 4 to 8.

Reinforcing this exhortation and providing an example for them, the apostle concludes, "Those things, which ye have both learned, and received, and heard, and seen in me, do: and the God of peace shall be with you." The full extent of his example to them in these important aspects of Christian life and character is itemized here. They had learned this through instruction from Paul; they had heard it with their ears, and they had seen it with their eyes. Now they were to, literally, "keep on practicing these things." The result would be that the God of peace would be with them. By this Paul was not implying that they would be forsaken of God if they fell short, but that rather the full experience of God's presence as the God of peace would be their portion, and with His presence would come the peace of God mentioned in verse 7.

In all of this, Paul's own painful situation of being a prisoner—with its many frustrations and limitations—gave him a platform on which to present his exhortation. If Paul could experience the peace of God as a prisoner, how much more should the Philippians be able to do so in their freedom? This portion of Scripture should often be in the mind and thinking of Christians in a troubled world with many troubled hearts.

PEACE IN REGARD TO THINGS, 4:10-13

The peace that passes understanding not only transforms the relationship to other Christians in the church and a Christian's own inner life, and assures peace of mind, but it helps a Christian to be adjusted to his circumstances and have peace in regard to things. There is no substitute for an intimate relationship with God as the source of spiritual power, as the secret of peace, and for experiencing such intimacy with God that the heart is transformed into a sanctuary of spiritual loveliness. When one is properly related to God and to the church and has achieved a measure of inner tranquility, he then is ready to face the challenge of life with its many cares. It was in this area that the Philippian church had been a special blessing to Paul, having ministered to his physical needs through their gifts and having facilitated his fellowship with them through their messenger, Epaphroditus. This had brought great joy to the apostle, and it gives him an occasion to comment on the Christian's attitude toward circumstances.

Paul says, "But I rejoiced in the Lord greatly, that now at the last your care of me hath flourished again; wherein ye were also careful, but ye lacked opportunity" (v. 10). The word for "rejoice" in the aorist tense in the Greek text signifies a specific experience of rejoicing. Although he had rejoiced many times over God's grace in the Philippian

church and had exhorted them repeatedly to "keep on rejoicing," using the present tense, here he is referring to a
specific experience of joy which had come to him when they
had shown their love for him by sending both an offering and
Epaphroditus to minister to him.

He adds to the thought of his rejoicing three descriptive
concepts. Immediately after the first word in the sentence,
"I rejoice," (Gk, *ècharen*), Paul introduces the conjunctive
particle *de* which could be translated "but," "and," "on the
other hand," or "also." The word *de* is used sometimes simply to add another thought, but frequently is found in the
sense of a contrast or an additional thought which might be
overlooked.[10] Lightfoot says, "The *de* arrests a subject which
is in danger of escaping: see Gal. iv.20."[11]

In speaking of the wonderful peace which the Lord had
given him, the apostle did not want to overlook the contribution the Philippian church had made to his well-being
and comfort. He adds also "in the Lord," indicating that
the entire circumstance was viewed as a part of the Lord's
dealings with him. He concludes by adding the adjective
megalos, meaning *greatly,* a word used only here in the New
Testament.

The occasion for this rejoicing was that the Philippian
church "now at the last"—after a passage of time from their
previous manifested interest—their care of thinking of him
(from a Greek word meaning "to think") had flourished
again. The word translated "flourished" (Gk, *anethalete*)
means literally "to grow" or "bloom again," as a plant previously dormant which puts forth new shoots and thereby
manifests new life.

To avoid the impression that he was being critical of de-
lay, he adds, "wherein ye were also careful," literally, "in
which also you were being thoughtful," referring to their

previous kindnesses to him. But any lack of solicitude on
their part had been occasioned by the fact that they "lacked
opportunity," a word found only here in the New Testament,
with the imperfect tense indicating that up to the present
time they were lacking this opportunity to serve him. On the
one hand they were not chargeable with any fault in not having previously helped him, but on the other hand their present opportunity which they had seized was most commenda-
ble and heartwarming to Paul.

To avoid any thought of being grasping concerning these
physical benefits which had come to him, he continues,
"Not that I speak in respect of want: for I have learned, in
whatsoever state I am, therewith to be content" (v. 11). He
did not want his commendation of them to be regarded as a
complaint that something was lacking, because, as he states,
through many experiences he had learned that his circumstances were by God's appointment and in them he should
be content. The word translated "want" is found only here
and in Mark 12:44 in the New Testament. Another rare
word is used for "content," a word also found in 2 Corinthians 9:8, where it is translated "sufficiency," and 1 Timothy 6:6, translated "contentment." In the philosophy of the
stoics, the word expresses self-sufficiency, not needing any
outside help. It is not contentment arising from an abundance of things, but an inner adjustment to outer circumstances. In Paul's case, this resulted from spiritual grace.

Then he continues to explain what he means: "I know
both how to be abased, and I know how to abound: every
where and in all things I am instructed both to be full and
to be hungry, both to abound and to suffer need" (v. 12).
He had "learned" (Gk, *emathon*) to be content. In expressing his knowledge of how to be abased and to abound, he
uses the Greek word *oida* in the sense of "understanding"

or "entering into the secret of." By being "abased" he refers to the humbling process of having very little. His knowledge of "how to abound" means to "have more than enough." He amplifies this by saying, "I am instructed," literally, "I have learned the secret of" how "to be full," that is, to be full of food, and how "to be hungry" as a by-product of poverty.

Paul then repeats what he just said, that he had learned "both to abound and to suffer need," this time stating it in reverse order but using the same Greek words. What he is saying is that whether in general circumstances, that is, the place in which he is staying, or the particular situation of his physical supply of food or lack of it, he had learned the secret of peace in the midst of such trials. If in these basic factors of life the apostle was adjusted to the will of God, it would be comparatively easy to accept the will of God in other matters.

All of this, however, was not accomplished through any special strength of Paul himself, and he is careful to give Christ the credit: "I can do all things through Christ which strengtheneth me" (v. 13). In this statement the word *all* is emphasized, coming first in the sentence; and two different words for strength or power are used. As Vincent points out, the "all" means "not only all the things just mentioned, but everything."[12] Translated literally, verse 13 is, "In all things I continue to be strong by the one empowering me." The best texts omit the word *Christ,* but of course this is the one to whom Paul referred. The secret of peace and the secret of contentment are inseparable from the experience of the sustaining power and grace of God. It was for this reason that Paul could be so content, even though chained to a guard and awaiting trial for his life. The secret which he discovered is what God wants every Christian to know: deliverance from dependence on things and circumstances, but complete dependence upon Christ. This, in a word, is peace.

PEACE IN REGARD TO CARE FOR OTHERS, 4:14-19

There is a real danger that Christians occupied with Christ and content in their own circumstances, however difficult, can thereby become careless about the needs of others. Although content with his lot, Paul does not follow the stoic philosophy that deprivation is necessarily good. There is no need for suffering for suffering's sake, and Christians who are indifferent to the needs of others on the ground that this is the circumstance in which God has placed them are not thinking straight.

The apostle accordingly commends the Philippians, "Notwithstanding ye have well done, that ye did communicate with my affliction" (v. 14). Although he would have been content to have remained in deprivation, even of the essentials of life, the Philippians did well in sharing with him and relieving his suffering. The common idea that servants of the Lord are somehow better off if they are poor and live on a lower economic level than others is not part of Paul's philosophy. There should be, instead, an equality, a sharing in which each takes into consideration the special needs of others.

The Philippian church was especially to be commended in their present act of giving because in this benefit to the apostle, as in their earlier care of him, they had been alone in such thoughtful sharing. He reminds them, "Now ye Philippians know also, that in the beginning of the gospel, when I departed from Macedonia, no church communicated with me as concerning giving and receiving, but ye only" (v. 15). Their financial support of Paul began early in his ministry after he had preached the gospel to them. Vincent points out that the expression "in the beginning of the gospel" "is clearly shown by the succeeding words to be to the first preaching of the gospel in Macedonia, about ten years before the composition of this letter. . . . He alludes, no doubt, to money supplied before or at his departure from Macedonia (Acts xvii.14)."[13]

Paul may be referring to this in 2 Corinthians 11:8-9:

> I robbed other churches, taking wages of them, to do you service. And when I was present with you, and wanted, I was chargeable to no man: for that which was lacking to me the brethren which came from Macedonia supplied: and in all things I have kept myself from being burdensome unto you, and so will I keep myself.

Although he refers to contributions as coming from "other churches," the implication is that those churches contributed to him when he was still in their area, while the Philippian church was commended because they sent offerings to him even when he was not present. More specifically he states, "For even in Thessalonica ye sent once and again unto my necessity" (v. 16; cf. evidence of Paul's poverty and need, 1 Th 2:9; 2 Th 3:8). This was all the more remarkable in view of his relatively brief time in Thessalonica. Geographically, of course, Thessalonica and Philippi were close together and connected by trade routes, and messages and offerings could have gone back and forth between the two cities in a relatively short period of time. Their intimate knowledge of his needs, as well as his location in Thessalonica, reflects the abiding interest of the Philippian church in Paul's missionary efforts.

Once again to avoid any thought of covetousness on his part, Paul says, "Not because I desire a gift: but I desire fruit that may abound to your account" (v. 17). As Lightfoot observes, "Again the Apostle's nervous anxiety to clear himself interposes. By thus enlarging on the past liberality of the Philippians, he might be thought to covet their gifts. This possible misapprehension he at once corrects."[14]

Ultimately Paul's joy was not simply in the benefit received; but like a parent who receives a gift from his child, he rejoices more in the fact that the child gives it than in the gift itself. His earnest desire for their spiritual progress and that they might be fruitful in the Lord's work is reflected in verse 17. The word translated "desire," repeated twice, is in the present tense and, translated literally, is "not because I am seeking a gift: but I am seeking fruit that may abound to your account." The word is found only here and in Romans 11:7 in the New Testament.

His contemplation of their gift and thoughtfulness brings forth from his overflowing heart a statement of the fullness of his joy: "But I have all, and abound: I am full, having received of Epaphroditus the things which were sent from you, an odour of a sweet smell, a sacrifice acceptable, well-pleasing to God" (v. 18). By this he means that he not only has supply of his temporal things, but that his heart and life are full of joy; his cup was overflowing. He describes their gift as a sweet-smelling sacrifice, such as the incense offered in the temple to the Lord (cf. 2 Co 2:15-16; Eph 5:2). It is also declared to be an acceptable sacrifice, as in Romans 12:1, and well pleasing to God, as in Hebrews 13:16 (cf. 1 Pe 2:5). The Word of God puts a high premium on thoughtful, loving gifts, especially when directed to those who are serving the Lord so well and suffering for Christ's sake. One's stewardship in temporal things is often a barometer of his spiritual condition, and thoughtfulness in sharing with others and in relieving their needs is a part of having the mind of Christ who gave so freely to us.

His discussion of giving and receiving temporal things as

an expression of the love and thoughtfulness of God now brings Paul to the great statement, "But my God shall supply all your need according to his riches in glory by Christ Jesus" (v. 19). Muller comments,

> "My God"—words vibrating with the ring of a personal testimony and confession of faith—"will supply every need of yours," will make provision in His fatherly love and care for all needs material and spiritual, for time and eternity, according to the richness and fulness of His divine providence.[15]

In a sense, every gift is an act of faith because, in many cases, justification could be found for retaining the gift for the selfish benefit of the donor. However, having shared with Paul and thus depriving themselves of what benefit their offering might have been to themselves, they also placed themselves in a faith relationship to God where they could in a special sense depend upon God's supply of their own needs. This would be in keeping with the riches to be found in the glory in Christ Jesus, that is, according to the infinite resources of God. Muller believes the expression "in glory" should be taken with the words "shall supply"; hence, "God will supply in glory, in a glorious manner."[16]

Although there is a seeming ellipsis in thought, what Paul is implying is that their need was not simply in the temporal realm, but also in the spiritual realm; and that God's total care of them would be in keeping with His infinite glory in heaven. His supply would be in view of their eternal benefit rather than simply their temporal needs.

Accordingly, God might permit suffering if suffering were what they needed. Or, God might permit lack of temporal things if this would be to their spiritual benefit. In all their circumstances, however, they could be assured that God was working actively on their part to provide triumph over anxiety. God was not lacking in power, but was infinitely wise in all of His supply of their needs.

CONCLUSION, 4:20-23

In completing the thought of verse 19, Paul begins his conclusion with the benediction, "Now unto God and our Father be glory for ever and ever. Amen." The same God and Father who would cause them to triumph in Christ would be the Recipient of glory in connection with all His dealings, both with Paul and with the Philippians. Ultimately the supreme test of every circumstance and every act on their part was whether it was to the glory of God. It was Paul's earnest desire that he bring glory to the Lord, and in this he wanted the Philippians to share.

Paul first of all salutes "every saint in Christ Jesus" (v. 21). By this he means that he is sending his greetings to them as individuals. As Alford points out, by "every saint" he means "every individual saint," as indicated by the singular number, in contrast to "all the saints," a collective term used in 4:22.[17] He also sends greetings from the other brethren who are with him in Rome, referring to his immediate circle of friends. He expands the list of those greeting them as including "all the saints," and then adds "chiefly they that are of Caesar's household" (v. 22). This refers to those who were working in Caesar's household, whether slaves or freemen; and the implication is that Paul, through his ministry in Rome, had won many of them to Jesus Christ. Here without comment is introduced one of the reasons why the apostle was rejoicing in his circumstances, however difficult. It gave him, as it were, access to the inner circle of Rome, those who were at the very heart of the military and political life of the city and the empire. It was a pulpit which he could not have achieved if he had sought it, but by circumstances he was given entrance to those who could be an important channel to many others in communicating the gospel.

This great epistle is brought to a close with the simple benediction, "The grace of our Lord Jesus Christ be with you all. Amen" (v. 23). The Christian life, which is an expression of grace, is by grace sustained, and the final verse to some extent summarizes all of Paul's yearnings for these Christians who had manifested their love and care for him.

Taken as a whole, the epistle to the Philippians contributes immeasurably to Christian doctrine and triumphant experience. In one sense it revolves around the principal characters—Paul, Timothy and Epaphroditus. In another sense it centers in the Philippian church, whose ten years of history were an epic in the grace of God. In the deepest sense, however, Christ is the center of this epistle. It is the mind of Christ, His love, His humiliation, His willingness to suffer, and His exaltation which constitute the supreme illustration of obedience to God, and the reminder that after suffering comes the glory. A proper relationship to the Lord Jesus Christ would bring about the experiencing of the mind of Christ by the Philippian church, with resulting unity and love for each other and the minimizing of internal conflicts and friction. In Christ also is found supremely the doctrine of grace—grace as a way of salvation and as a way of life—in contrast to the Judaizing teaching which Paul rebukes, and in even sharper contrast to the antinomian sects which have not apprehended the grace of God at all.

Above all, the apostle wants the Philippian church to experience triumphant peace—peace among themselves, peace of heart, peace of mind, and peace in relation to earthly things and circumstances. In this his exhortation is an extension of his own experience and his own triumph.

The closing benediction, "The grace of our Lord Jesus Christ be with you all," far more than a customary benediction gathers in all the intensive meaning of the exhortation of the preceding chapters. It was a deeper apprehension of grace which was the key to all that Paul yearned for in the Philippian church. The epistle which began with grace and peace in 1:2, now ends with the final prayer for grace which climaxes a chapter dedicated to peace.

The warmth of this epistle and its relevance to the intimate, spiritual conflicts of all ages, has made this letter of Paul timeless, not only because it is Scripture but because it relates so accurately to the spiritual needs of Christians in all circumstances of life. Paul's epistle to the Philippians is his epistle to the church of Jesus Christ, a treasure-house of truth and a means by which a Christian not only can exalt Christ but also can find the deepest and richest experiences of triumphant walking with the Lord.

NOTES

INTRODUCTION

1. Cf. J. B. Lightfoot, *St. Paul's Epistle to the Philippians,* pp. 74-77; J. J. Muller, *The Epistles of Paul to the Philippians and to Philemon,* pp. 14-17; William Hendriksen, *A Commentary on the Epistle to the Philippians,* pp. 31-36.
2. Henry C. Thiessen, *Introduction to the New Testament,* pp. 247-49; cf. Lightfoot, pp. 74-75.
3. For an extended discussion of the order of the epistles of the captivity, see Lightfoot, pp. 30-46. Hendriksen, pp. 30-31, places Philippians last, as do many others.
4. F. C. Synge, *Philippians and Colossians,* p. 12.
5. Ibid., p. 13.
6. Donald Guthrie, *The Pauline Epistles,* p. 153; cf. pp. 148-53.
7. Synge, p. 13.
8. Lightfoot, pp. 99-104; Hendriksen, pp. 21-31.
9. Lightfoot, pp. 171-78.
10. Ibid., pp. 1-29.
11. Ibid., p. 14.
12. Thiessen, p. 226.
13. Lightfoot, p. 16.
14. Ibid., pp. 47-65; cf. also the graphic account by Hendriksen, pp. 4-7.
15. Lightfoot, p. 59.
16. Ibid., p. 60.
17. Ibid., p. 65.
18. Ibid., p. 76.
19. Guthrie, p. 144.

CHAPTER 1

1. Marvin R. Vincent, *A Critical and Exegetical Commentary on the Epistles to the Philippians and to Philemon,* pp. 1-2.
2. J. B. Lightfoot, *St. Paul's Epistles to the Philippians,* pp. 59-60. Cf. Ac 19:21; 20:1-3, 5-6; 1 Co 16:5-6; 2 Co 1:15-17; 2:12 ff.; 7:5-6; 8:1; 9:2-4.
3. William F. Arndt and F. Wilbur Gingrich, *A Greek-English Lexicon of the New Testament,* pp. 7-8.
4. A. R. Fausset in Robert Jamieson, A. R. Fausset and David Brown, *A Commentary Critical, Experimental and Practical on the Old and New Testaments,* 6:424.
5. John Calvin, *Commentaries on the Epistles of Paul the Apostle to the Philippians, Colossians, and Thessalonians,* p. 23. Cf. J. J. Muller, *The Epistles of Paul to the Philippians and to Philemon,* p. 35.

6. Lightfoot offers an extended dissertation on "The Christian Ministry" which deals with the officers of the church (pp. 181-269), showing how the original synonymous character of bishops and presbyters was gradually changed in church history. Cf. also Arndt and Gingrich, pp. 183, 299, 706-7; and Donald Guthrie, *The Pauline Epistles*, pp. 140-41, 213-16.

7. J. H. Harrop, "Epistle," *The New Bible Dictionary*, J. D. Douglas, ed., pp. 383-84.

8. Lightfoot, p. 84.

9. F. B. Meyer, *The Epistle to the Philippians*, p. 22.

10. Lightfoot, p. 86.

11. Arndt and Gingrich, p. 24.

12. Lightfoot, p. 86.

13. William Hendriksen, *A Commentary on the Epistle to the Philippians*, pp. 61-62.

14. Lightfoot, p. 88; cf. pp. 7-19.

15. Ibid., p. 88.

16. J. J. Muller, *The Epistles of Paul to the Philippians and to Philemon*, pp. 88-89.

17. Lightfoot, p. 89.

18. Ibid., p. 91.

19. Guy H. King, *Joy Way*, p. 34.

20. Meyer, pp. 40-41.

21. Cf. Muller, pp. 65-66.

22. Arndt and Gingrich, p. 901.

23. Cf. Lightfoot, p. 106; Muller, p. 70.

Chapter 2

1. J. B. Lightfoot, *St. Paul's Epistle to the Philippians*, p. 107.

2. William F. Arndt and F. Wilbur Gingrich, *A Greek-English Lexicon of the New Testament*, p. 626.

3. Lightfoot, p. 107.

4. *Agape* is the deepest word for divine love.

5. F. B. Meyer, *The Epistle to the Philippians*, p. 54.

6. Arndt and Gingrich, p. 530.

7. William Hendriksen, *A Commentary on the Epistle to the Philippians*, p. 104.

8. Cf. Lightfoot, special article on "The Synonymes *Morphe* and *Schema*," pp. 127-33.

9. Ibid., p. 112.

10. Ibid.

11. Cf. Hendriksen, p. 104.

12. John Calvin, *Commentaries on the Epistles of Paul the Apostle to the Philippians, Colossians, and Thessalonians*, pp. 58-59.

13. Ibid., p. 59.

14. Cf. Lightfoot, pp. 113-15.

15. Ibid., p. 115.

16. J. J. Muller, *The Epistles of Paul to the Philippians and to Philemon*, pp. 88-89.

17. Ibid., p. 88.

18. Cf. Ibid., p. 89.

19. Arndt and Gingrich, p. 422.

20. Muller, p. 91.

21. Meyer, p. 77.
22. Hendriksen, pp. 123-24.
23. F. C. Synge, *Philippians and Colossians*, p. 36.
24. Lightfoot, p. 118.
25. Cf. ibid., pp. 122-23.
26. Ibid., p. 123.
27. Hendriksen, p. 142.

CHAPTER 3

1. Robert H. Mounce in *The Wycliffe Bible Commentary*, Charles F. Pfeiffer and Everett F. Harrison, eds., p. 1327.
2. J. B. Lightfoot, *St. Paul's Epistle to the Philippians*, p. 142.
3. For the full discussion, see ibid., pp. 138-42. See also J. J. Muller, *Epistles of Paul to the Philippians and to Philemon*, p. 105.
4. William Hendriksen, *A Commentary to the Epistle to the Philippians*, p. 149.
5. Muller, pp. 107-8.
6. Lightfoot, p. 146.
7. Hendriksen, p. 163.
8. Lightfoot, p. 148.
9. A. R. Fausset in Robert Jamieson, A. R. Fausset and David Brown, *A Commentary Critical, Experimental, and Practical on the Old and New Testaments*, 6:434.
10. W. E. Vine, *The Epistles to the Philippians and Colossians*, p. 83.
11. Charles J. Ellicott, *A Critical and Grammatical Commentary on St. Paul's Epistles to the Philippians, Colossians, and Philemon*, p. 87.
12. Ibid., p. 86.
13. Fausset, p. 434.
14. Muller, p. 125.
15. Vine, p. 86.
16. Lightfoot, pp. 154-55.
17. Vine, p. 88.
18. Cf. Muller, pp. 130-32.
19. William F. Arndt and F. Wilbur Gingrich, *A Greek-English Lexicon of the New Testament*, pp. 692-93.
20. Hendriksen, p. 183.

CHAPTER 4

1. Cf. J. B. Lightfoot, *St. Paul's Epistle to the Philippians*, p. 157.
2. J. J. Muller, *The Epistles of Paul to the Philippians and to Philemon*, pp. 138-39.
3. Lightfoot, p. 158. Lightfoot goes on to discuss the other alternative meanings, including the possibility that it is a proper name.
4. Ibid., pp. 159-60.
5. Marvin R. Vincent, *The Epistles to the Philippians and to Philemon*, p. 133.
6. W. F. Arndt and F. W. Gingrich, *A Greek-English Lexicon of the New Testament*, p. 292.
7. Vincent, pp. 134-35.
8. Muller, p. 142.

9. Arndt and Gingrich, p. 477.
10. Ibid., p. 170.
11. Lightfoot, p. 163.
12. Vincent, p. 145.
13. Ibid., p. 147.
14. Lightfoot, p. 166.
15. Muller, p. 152.
16. Ibid.
17. Henry Alford, *The Greek Testament*, 3:195.

BIBLIOGRAPHY

Alford, Henry. *The Greek New Testament.* With revision by Everett F. Harrison. Vol. 3. Chicago: Moody, 1958.

Arndt, William F. and Gingrich, F. Wilbur. *A Greek-English Lexicon of the New Testament.* Chicago: U. of Chicago, 1957.

Calvin, John. *Commentaries on the Epistles of Paul the Apostle to the Philippians, Colossians, and Thessalonians.* Translated and edited from the original Latin, and collated with the French version by John Pringle. Edinburg: Calvin Trans. Soc., 1851.

Douglas, James Dixon, ed. *The New Bible Dictionary.* Grand Rapids: Eerdmans, 1965.

Ellicott, Charles John. *A Critical and Grammatical Commentary on St. Paul's Epistles to the Philippians, Colossians, and Philemon.* Andover: Draper, 1876.

Godet, Frederic. *Studies on the Epistles of Paul.* Translated by Annie Harwood Holmden. New York: Doran, n.d.

Guthrie, Donald. *The Pauline Epistles.* Chicago: Inter-Varsity, 1963.

Harrop, J. H. *The New Bible Dictionary.* Edited by J. D. Douglas. Grand Rapids: Eerdmans, 1965.

Hendriksen, William. *A Commentary on the Epistle to the Philippians.* London: Banner of Truth Trust, 1963.

Jamieson, Robert; Fausset, Andrew R.; and Brown, David. *A Commentary, Critical, Experimental, and Practical, on the Old and New Testaments.* Vol. 6. Glasgow: Collins, 1874.

Johnstone, Robert. *Lectures Exegetical and Practical on the Epistle of Paul to the Philippians.* Grand Rapids: Baker, 1955.

Kelly, William. *Lectures on Philippians and Colossians.* Denver: Wilson Foundation, n.d.

King, Guy Hope. *Joy Way.* Fort Washington, Pa.: Christian Literature Crusade, 1952.

Lightfoot, Joseph Barber. *St. Paul's Epistle to the Philippians.* Revised text with introduction, notes and dissertations of 1953 ed. (reprinted from original ed., London: Macmillan, 1913). Grand Rapids: Zondervan, 1968.

Martin, Ralph Philip. *The Epistle of Paul to the Philippians.* Grand Rapids: Eerdmans, 1959.

Meyer, Frederick Brotherton. *The Epistle to the Philippians.* Grand Rapids: Zondervan, 1952.

Muller, Jacobus Johannes. *The Epistles of Paul to the Philippians and to Philemon.* Grand Rapids: Eerdmans, 1955.

Moule, Handley Carr Glynn. *Philippian Studies.* London: Hodder & Stoughton, 1897.

Nicoll, William Robertson, ed. *The Expositor's Bible.* London: Hodder & Stoughton, 1893.

Noble, Frederick A. *Discourses on Philippians.* New York: Revell, 1896.

Pfeiffer, Charles F. and Harrison, Everett F., eds. *The Wycliffe Bible Commentary.* Chicago: Moody, 1962.

Robertson, Archibald Thomas. *Word Pictures in the New Testament.* Vol. 4: *The Epistles of Paul.* Nashville: Sun. Sch. Bd. of Sthrn. Bap. Con., 1931.

Strauss, Lehman. *Devotional Studies in Philippians.* New York: Loizeaux, 1959.

Synge, Francis Charles. *Philippians and Colossians.* London: S. C. M., 1951.

Thiessen, Henry Clarence. *Introduction to the New Testament.* Grand Rapids: Eerdmans, 1943.

Unger, Merrill Frederick. *Unger's Bible Dictionary.* Chicago: Moody, 1957.

Vincent, Marvin R. *A Critical and Exegetical Commentary on* the Epistles to the Philippians and to Philemon. New York: Scribner, 1903.

Vine, William Edwy. *Epistles to the Philippians and Colossians.* London: Oliphants, 1955.

Wuest, Kenneth Samuel. *Philippians in the Greek New Testament.* Grand Rapids: Eerdmans, 1942; 9th printing, 1959.